"*Ilahinoor: Awakening the Divine Human* is a well-woven journey drawn from prevailing scientific theory, ancient mythology, and personal experience. Kiara Windrider effortlessly combines multi-cultural threads into a rich tapestry of hope and practical application. This is truly a comprehensive guide to understanding and awakening our divine expression."

— Lisa Wimberger, Author of *New Beliefs, New Brain*

"*Ilahinoor* is a synthesis of right and left brain understanding of upcoming Earth and consciousness changes, as well as a practical method to help us through those changes. Kiara's journey has been an adventure story in itself, one that has taken him to a visionary perspective that he embodies with gentleness and humility."

— Mary Lou Johnson, Founder,
Canadian Holistic Nurses Association

"The strength and flow of my Source connection has been greatly enhanced by my experiences with Ilahinoor."

— Kimberley Jones, "The Energy Whisperer" and
Author of *Soul Whispers*

"In this remarkable, objective, and soothing exploration of the exciting times we live in, Kiara Windrider allows us to directly experience the evolutionary shift in consciousness that is our personal and planetary destiny, mediated by a galactic light now flowing through us. Kiara refers to this galactic field as Ilahinoor, and with the customary clarity and simplicity that marks him and his writings, he shows us how we can each consciously connect with this field, ascending in consciousness even as the Light descends into our body and transforms it. Pay close attention: Ilahinoor is the light-line from the Divine here to save us from extinction."

— Nilima Bhat, Founder/Director of Sampurnah - The
Wholeness Practice (Sampurnah.com)

"Ilahinoor is a truly precious and powerful gift for those yearning to receive and integrate Kiara Windrider's guidance on their journey for spiritual awakening and wisdom surrounding the planet's shifting process."

> — Alexandra Delis-Abrams, Ph.D., Author of *Attitudes, Beliefs, and Choices*

"How amazing to find ourselves in this momentous time in history. Despair often seems our only choice of response, but Kiara Windrider provides us with some of the most inspiring and hopeful navigational tools we will find anywhere. His work is well researched, poetic, and beautifully written. You will not find a more exciting guide to our planetary future — and most exciting is that under his gentle guidance, we can all be participants in this galactic wave of re-birth."

> — Carol and John Wiebe, Educators and Peace/Environmental Activists

"Having conducted Ilahinoor groups and teleconferences for over four years, we are continually impressed by how powerfully it catalyzes the embodiment of the Divine Light. There is nothing of greater importance at this crucial evolutionary time than continuing to raise the quotient of the Living Light we embody."

> — Barry Martin Snyder, Evolutionary Catalyst and Co-Author of *Birthing the Luminous Self*

"This book offers welcome practical advice about how one can actually energetically prepare for the biggest change that humanity has ever experienced. Here's how to anticipate and be prepared."

> — John L. Petersen, Editor of FUTUREdition and Author of *A Vision for 2012: Planning for Extraordinary Change*

ilahinoor

AWAKENING THE DIVINE HUMAN

KIARA WINDRIDER

DIVINE
ARTS

Published by DIVINE ARTS
DivineArtsMedia.com

An imprint of Michael Wiese Productions
12400 Ventura Blvd. # 1111
Studio City, CA 91604
(818) 379-8799, (818) 986-3408 (Fax)
www.mwp.com

Cover design by Johnny Ink *www.johnnyink.com*
Cover Art: Rodrigo Adolfo
Model: www.Saragath-Stock.deviantart.com
Copyediting by Annalisa Zox-Weaver
Book Layout by Gina Mansfield
Dorina Maciejka – illustrations (dorinam@wp.pl)
          Blog: dorinamaciejkailustruje.blogsp.com
Roger Uhrig – diagrams (r.uhrig@gmx.de)

Printed by McNaughton & Gunn, Inc., Saline, Michigan
Manufactured in the United States of America

Library of Congress Cataloging-in-Publication Data

Windrider, Kiara.
Ilahinoor : awakening the divine human / Kiara Windrider.
    p. cm.
ISBN 978-1-61125-010-7
1. Spiritual life--Miscellanea. I. Title.
BF1999.W632 2012
204--dc23
                                   2011039290

CONTENTS

ACKNOWLEDGEMENTS

I wish to acknowledge some of the forces permeating the Ilahinoor field:

The Galactic Mother, who drives solar and planetary evolution

Our Earth Mother Gaia in her own journey of awakening

The whales and dolphins who inhabit Gaia's oceans

Earth dragons, elohim, and the elemental spirits of nature

Helpers from the angelic and archangelic realms

Ascended Masters who have been guiding our collective journey

The field of Supramental Light anchored by Mother and Sri Aurobindo

The mystery schools and neters of ancient Egypt

Sufi traditions inspired by Mevlana Jelaluddin Rumi

Ordinary humans willing to share the Light with open hearts

The One Spirit that Moves through All Things

To the Divine Mother in all her forms

And to the mother who birthed me into this life,

I dedicate this book.

FOREWORD

Kimberley Jones

*"Let your heart's light guide you to my house.
Let your heart's light show you that we are one."*

— Rumi

As foreseen by the ancients, we are waking from a long dark night of separation and materialism, emerging into an integral, interconnected worldview. Our sun is now in alignment with the Galactic Center. The evolutionary pulse from our Great Mother is reverberating through our consciousness, bathing us in Source energy, awakening us to the infinite possibilities of our quantum, fractal, and holographic reality. Waves of high-frequency cosmic and gamma rays are lapping at our shores, affecting physical matter as well as how we think and feel.

We are evolving. We are expanding. We are remembering.

Conscious Evolutionary thinker Barbara Marx Hubbard refers to this process as the birth of the Universal Human. The labor pains are evident. Old systems and power bases are crumbling into chaos. But the pain has meaning. As our inner and outer foundations are shaken to the core, we are being reborn through post-traumatic growth and spiritual transformation. We are awakening.

The Great Mother of our Galactic Center is blasting our planet and our consciousness with intense frequencies of Light, activating our divine blueprint. Anything not in alignment with our highest evolutionary impulse (LOVE) is being challenged and broken down. We either flow with it or feel the pain of resisting the inevitable.

This process of breaking down could be referred to as a healing crisis. I have seen a personal version of this planetary process in myself and in clients over the years. The Light pours in, and old pain from what Eckhart Tolle refers to as the personal or collective "pain body" is brought to the surface. Anything not in alignment with the Light is challenged and brought up to be transmuted. As this old stored information comes up, we are called to be witness and observer of the process. We are invited to no longer act out or project this pain onto each other, causing destruction, but to trust the process, align with our heart, and remember who we are; LOVE in physical form.

We must gather our scattered, separated selves and reconnect with our eternal soul. Old paradigms on Earth are weakening and crumbling. It is time for compassion and communication over conflict, collaboration rather than competition, and transparency and integrity over concealment. The evolutionary fuel for this shift is LOVE.

When we open our hearts wide enough and surrender completely, we become a conduit for grounding the Light of Source to Earth, blessing all. Kiara Windrider is one such person. I have received Ilahinoor from Kiara personally, and it has been a blessing in my life. His cosmic download is a gift, a Light language offered to all and to be used and shared by all. As Ilahinoor opens us as toroidal conduits of energy to and from the universe, we become the place where heaven and earth meet and make love.

Kiara is a chosen midwife for the Great Mother to give birth to the next phase of our consciousness. In the pages that follow, you will not only learn about the nourishing, grounding energy of Ilahinoor and how Kiara came to birth it to Earth, but you will also receive it. In holding this book, you will be bathed in its frequency, affecting you and everyone you meet in the process. Consciousness is contagious, and this book is a catalyst for a new epidemic of enlightenment.

———o———

Kimberley Jones, BA (Hons), is **an energy-intuitive, soul guide, 4th-generation seer**, and author of *Soul Whispers*. Her passion and mission at this challenging and exciting time on Earth is to inspire and empower the next wave of awakening creative **souls** in readiness for the world changes that are upon us. Learn more at KimberleyJones.com.

PREFACE – A DREAM

There is an old story about the man who dreams he is a butterfly. The dream is so vivid that when he wakes up, he is not clear whether he is a man who dreamed he was a butterfly, or a butterfly now dreaming he is a man.

Perhaps this parable is appropriate for this age. There is a sense of dream-like absurdity about these times. All around us is a world of time and space that we believe to be real. We struggle to survive in this world, we grapple with relationships, and we yearn to lift ourselves out of unfulfilling lives of quiet desperation. We look around at a world gone out of control, careening rapidly toward chaos and madness, and wonder how long we have before some cosmic clock begins to toll our final hour of existence.

Meanwhile, in some distant corner of our minds, a new reality intrudes. It tells us that there is more to existence than we are currently aware of, more to our world than we can experience with our physical senses. It whispers to us its song of hope rather than fear, excitement rather than doom. Like a caterpillar dreaming an unknown dream, this reality hints of worlds waiting beyond a distant horizon, wilder than anything we've known.

How do we distinguish between wishful dreams born of existential despair and true dreams birthed from an awakening consciousness? Are we human beings who once dreamed of a golden age only to awaken to the nightmare we have created around us? Or, are we awakening now within this dream to real possibilities as yet unknown? Are we butterflies in disguise?

This is the theme I wish to explore in this book. There is a light emerging from the darkness of this age, a light shining strong and bright from within. It is a light that can be accessed by each one of us as an antidote to deep webs of subconscious programming and fear that have kept us trapped in illusion. We have mistaken this illusion for reality, and constructed our lives around maintaining the illusion.

The waves of light moving toward us now are designed to penetrate this subconscious programming and to awaken us from the dream. I refer to this light as Ilahinoor. My quest to understand what this light is about, where it emerges from, and why it is moving through our consciousness at this time in planetary history, has led me through some amazing experiences and insights into a field of immense hope for humanity and the world.

I would like to share this journey with you. It is a cocreative journey, and I am aware that my own journey into healing and awakening is not separate from yours. It is my hope that what you receive from this book is not merely a deeper understanding of what our planetary journey is about, but also a powerful, deeply felt, cellular transmission of this Ilahinoor light that propels each of you into a quantum shift of awakening!

PART I

THE BIG PICTURE

We shall not cease from exploration
And the end of all our exploring
Will be to arrive where we started
And know the place for the first time.

— T.S. Eliot, *Little Gidding*

I wish to start by exploring the larger context for the Ilahinoor work, including addressing information about immense changes we may shortly be experiencing within our planetary experience. Although this summary is very short, some readers may wish to skip this part and go right into the Ilahinoor work. Readers who wish to explore this planetary experience in greater depth are urged to examine my earlier book *Year Zero: Time of the Great Shift*, in which you will find additional details as well as supporting documentation.

chapter 1

A Galactic Heartbeat

We are now awakening from a dream. The dream has become a nightmare of sorts, as we humans come ever closer to destroying our planetary home. But in the midst of the terrors we have unleashed, and cataclysms we might face in times to come, I also sense a hope, a hope that touches each of us, a hope that goes beyond wishful thinking to embrace a future potential bigger than anything I could have foreseen in years past. This hope is what I wish to share in this book.

My vision of reality is based on cycles of time that interweave, creating new universes. These are regular cycles, and therefore predictable. My view of reality is also based on the understanding that we are living simultaneously in multiple dimensions of existence, and that our ability to navigate among these dimensions is currently evolving.

I do not believe that the universe was simply created in a *big bang* at the beginning of time and space. I believe that we are undergoing a process of creation that continues, and that periodic events stimulate new cycles of creation. I sense that we are entering one such period of creation right here and now.

Furthermore, I believe that the universe is alive in the same way that we consider ourselves to be alive. It has a destiny of its own, spawning new worlds and dimensions in a continuous attempt to allow its own consciousness to evolve. One aspect of the universe is beyond space and time — which we might refer to as The Universe or Creator. There is also an aspect of the universe constructed within multiple dimensions of time and space, which we might refer to as Creation. Creator and Creation coexist in a continuous dance of discovery and exploration. Our destiny is to touch both of these realms, and to become cocreators of a new Earth.

In my earlier book, *Year Zero: Time of the Great Shift*,[1] I went through a detailed exploration of what Paul LaViolette, Ph.D., astrophysicist and author of *Earth Under Fire*,[2] refers to as a *galactic superwave*. Galactic superwaves are emanations of cosmic radiation that pulse out from the center of galaxies, streaming out through interstellar space in a more or less regular fashion. We can imagine this action as a galactic heartbeat, radiating cosmic ray particles and gamma ray particles throughout the Milky Way on a periodic basis.

In our own solar system, this pulse seems to be synchronized with cycles within our Sun, and cycles within the Earth. For reasons that I explain more fully in my previous book, our galactic heartbeat seems to move out in pulses approximately 12,000 years apart.[3] It may also be, as theorized by Douglas Vogt in his book *God's Day of Judgment: The Real Cause of Global Warming*,[4] that this 12,000-year pulse is a universal constant, and that all galaxies are synchronized to this heartbeat of life.

This galactic heartbeat is the driving force behind evolution. LaViolette asserts that rather than being birthed in one Big Bang of primal creation, the universe is continually birthing itself anew within the centers of galaxies. Galactic superwaves are carriers for these creative energies, igniting the forces of new creation wherever they travel. Every time a galactic superwave moves through our own solar system, a new cycle of evolution begins.

Indeed, a new cycle may be beginning right now.

chapter 2

Planetary Cycles

How did the universe come into being? Many a night as a young child, I would look up at the stars and find myself wondering how it all got here. There weren't so many words or concepts then, just a feeling of endless mystery and awe. Later, throughout my high school years, I learned to engage in endless debates between creationists and evolutionists. Creationists believe that divine intelligence set the entire universe into motion in one grand creative act in the beginning of all time. Evolutionists disregard the idea of divine intelligence and assert that the universe evolved by chance in a slow process of natural selection and genetic mutation.

Perhaps I lost a little bit of the mystery as I got caught up in the debate. Debates are about winning or losing, and someone has to be wrong in order for the other person to be right. But sooner or later, I started wondering if there might not be a third choice, a perspective that could hold and reconcile these opposing viewpoints.

I began to explore the idea of a *creative evolution*, which to me made much more sense than some kind of creator god suddenly creating everything out of nothing, or some mindless evolutionary force that went through infinite permutations of blind and desperate chance in order to create this miracle of beauty we call life. Couldn't a Divine Creator use the mechanism of evolution to create life and order in the universe?

This perspective has evolved for me over the years. As I began to disengage from the dogmas that often weigh heavily on both religious and scientific worldviews, a new understanding of creator and creation began to emerge — an understanding that we are not separate from either, and that we are active participants rather than passive observers in a constantly unfolding creation. I began to recognize that a field of divine intelligence permeates all things, and that new creation happens whenever this divine intelligence steps forcefully into the field of matter.

As I explored these questions further, I kept returning to the idea of the *galactic superwave*. It had a kind of mystical feel to it, and touched me in a place that words could not. LaViolette refers to the galactic center as a *Mother Star*; the Mayas referred to this creative womb as *Hunab Ku*. If I wanted to penetrate this mystery, I would need the insights of both science and ancient wisdom; I knew I had to follow this path.

What was the mechanism for creative evolution? I asked myself. And, is there a way we could participate more consciously in this new creation? Equally important, is it possible that we might be experiencing a wave of creative evolution in our own lifetimes, which could transform everything in our known universe?

More insights followed, and pieces of this cosmic jigsaw puzzle started to come together. The more I explored this process of creative evolution, the more I realized that we as humans — and we as a planet — are also part of this galactic wave. Nothing that happens out there is separate from our own thoughts and intentions. These insights led me to recognize that a field of light permeating and surrounding us is directly synchronized to the incoming galactic superwave. I realized that this phenomenon was an evolutionary wave that could carry us into the cauldron of a new creation — and that the only thing that holds us back from experiencing this wave is the density of our belief systems.

Right now, a field of light is entering our consciousness and can transform everything we have ever known — including this density of subconscious conditioning. As I share later in this book, we can each have access to this field and each feel the power of this light. If we can really and truly understand this phenomenon, then we need no longer perceive ourselves as powerless victims living in a world gone out of control. We become, instead, the wide-browed creators of a new Earth birthing itself through our wildest dreams!

The evolutionary mechanism begins right in the center of our galaxy. The creation of matter and energy that takes place during a galactic pulse is also an *information wave* coded with Creator-Consciousness. We, as human beings, not only inhabit bodies of matter but are also capable of attuning to this Creator-Consciousness. We are a bridge between creator and creation and, as such, have a part to play in the new creation.

So, what is the next step in the evolutionary mechanism? As successive superwaves emanating from the galactic center periodically move through our solar system, the intensity of this radiation overloads the protective plasma shield (known as the *heliopause*) surrounding our solar system. This shield gives way for a moment, letting in vast amounts of *cosmic dust* that are normally found orbiting outside our solar system in our journey through space.

Most of this cosmic dust is gravitationally attracted to the Sun and planetary bodies, initiating a cycle of intense activity within the solar system. Nuclear activity within the Sun is intensified, culminating in giant *solar flares* ejecting out into interplanetary space. Occasionally, an entire shell of the Sun gets ejected out in massive flares known as *coronal mass ejections*. CMEs can reach out and engulf an entire planet, including Earth, causing extreme magnetic fluctuations, and even what is known as *geomagnetic reversals*.

In his book *Magnetic Reversals and Evolutionary Leaps*,[1] Robert Felix reveals a connection between peaks in solar activity and the reversal of Earth's geomagnetic field, a phenomenon whereby the magnetic north and south poles of Earth switch places. Studies of ice core samples and fossil history indicate that these geomagnetic reversals are actually a recurring phenomenon in Earth's history. Although the period leading up to a reversal may be relatively gradual, these studies reveal that the actual reversal could happen in a matter of days — or even hours.

What happens during a geomagnetic reversal? The geomagnetic field of the Earth generates a magnetic shield extending hundreds of kilometers out into space and is known as the *Van Allen* belts. Just as the heliopause surrounding our solar system is designed to keep out interstellar dust as we journey through the galaxy, the Van Allen belts are designed to shield our planet from the intense cosmic radiation constantly passing through our solar system.

However, during a geomagnetic reversal, the Earth's magnetic field collapses, which, in turn, leads to the collapse of the Van Allen belts. In the absence of this magnetic shielding, huge storms of cosmic radiation rain down upon the Earth hundreds of times stronger than normal.

Thus, in this final phase of the evolutionary sequence, an *information wave* of high frequency cosmic rays and gamma rays moves through the field of life and matter on our planet. This wave is the same radiation that started off as a galactic superwave from the center of our galaxy, encoded with the power of creation. Responding to a field of light morphogenetically generated by this cosmic radiation, mutations happen. Some species go extinct. New species are birthed.

Unlike the Darwinian model of evolution, which holds that evolution is slow and gradual, this model of creative evolution postulates that these mutations happen very quickly in quantum jumps of new creation — *and that a field of intelligence guides this process.*

chapter 3

Geomagnetic Reversals

If evolutionary leaps and geomagnetic reversals are linked, as Robert Felix and a number of other researchers have claimed, indications suggest that our planet may be very close to making its next evolutionary leap. Although scientists cannot tell us precisely when such a shift would occur, a growing consensus is that it could be soon. Not only is the geomagnetic field of Earth decreasing very rapidly, but also the actual north and south poles of the planet are shifting quite dramatically — another sign that a geomagnetic reversal could be imminent.

The National Oceanic and Atmospheric Administration (NOAA) is a federal agency created to study oceanographic and atmospheric data. Their National Geophysical Data Center maintains a data set of annual magnetic north pole coordinates going back to the year 1590. In correlating all this data, the NOAA has come to the startling realization that the north pole of the Earth is on the move, and that the rate of this movement is increasing exponentially.

During the past 150 years, this rate of movement has more than doubled every fifty years. When this report was published around 2010, researchers noticed that there was almost as much movement in the ten years from 2000 to 2010 as in the forty-year period before that, and as much movement from 1960 to 2000 as in the hundred years prior to that. Furthermore, in the past 150 years, the pole has been moving in the same direction, indicating that the Earth's magnetic axis may be getting ready to flip. It is currently travelling at the rate of fifty-five to seventy kilometers every year in the direction of Siberia.[1]

More indications for the timing of this shift can be found in ancient mythologies and calendar systems. It seems clear to me that many prophecies and calendar systems were based on a study of cosmic cycles, perhaps even synchronized in some way with the galactic heartbeat.

The Mayan calendar has been at the forefront of people's consciousness for some time now. Many seem obsessed with global cataclysms related to the end date of this prophetic calendar, whatever that might be, without fully understanding the context for these events. The Mayas were attuned to a galactic consciousness, which they referred to as Hunab Ku. Their calendar, perhaps based on even earlier systems of time-keeping, represents a time when this galactic consciousness would once again intersect with human consciousness. I believe this event has to do with the incoming galactic superwave and its direct impact on our solar system and planet Earth.

For the Mayas, the focus of their prophetic calendar is not on cataclysm, doom, and gloom, but on the possibilities of a new beginning, an event that they refer to as *Year Zero*. During a travel trip to Guatemala in November 2009, I had the opportunity to meet Don Alejandro Cirilo and his wife, Elisabeth Araujo, who represent the Mayan Council of Elders.

They did not wish to be drawn into questions regarding specific dates for the ending of their calendar system. They said, however, that thirteen prophecies had been passed down through the generations regarding our journey into *Year Zero*, the time of new beginnings for the Earth. And they indicated that this event would be happening very soon!

When pressed for details about these thirteen prophecies, Don Alejandro simply said that twelve of those prophecies had already come to pass, and were thus not so relevant anymore. The thirteenth prophecy was yet to come, however, and would immediately precede Year Zero. This prophecy had to do with three days of darkness. He further added that when we begin to experience this event, we should not go into fear, but simply be grateful to the Creator and celebrate, for we have long awaited this time — this time when the veil between Creator and Creation would dissolve.

The following is taken from a speech Don Alejandro gave in Santa Fe, New Mexico in September 1999. A specific date for Year Zero was given in this speech, which I have left out, given his later insistence that we not focus too heavily on specific dates:

---○---

Heart of heaven, heart of the Earth, heart of the air, heart of the water...

Thank you, Father, for having given us life, bless us all, those who are here on Earth. Thank you, Father, bless our people, our mountains, our rivers, our lakes, all that we are, thank you, Father.

Honorable elders, beloved people, you who hear me, I bring this message, and also a greeting to all who hear this voice, here is Wakatel Utiw, Wandering Wolf, the voice of the forest, and the messenger of the Maya, who has shared with the seven races that cover the planet Earth. I have come in fulfillment of the prophecies; that we may all walk together, no group shall be left behind. I am here in fulfillment of this prophecy, carrying this message to all that hear me and to all who love the Earth, to all who love peace, and who love themselves. We are all living beings. A tree is a life and it is an elder, the same as a human being. A plant, while it is green, is a life. The smallest animal is a life that is part of the life of human beings. The rocks have spirit. The volcanoes and mountains have spirit. The rivers, oceans, and lakes have spirit. They are all children of the Father.

This is why I have come. I am the voice of the forest, the messenger of the Maya. I come to invite you to defend our Mother Earth and see that we continue to love the beauty of this great woman. We are millions and millions of human beings and we are destroying her. We are mistreating her. We are denuding and polluting her. When the Mother Earth is no longer suitable, our life will be worthless. We are creating our own misfortune, our own death.

The Mayan Prophecies tell us it is time to awaken, time for the dawn, so that the people will have peace and will be happy. The Mayan Prophecies also tell us... that what we are seeking, what we have to find, at last we have found it. We are here on Earth, where we want to be. This time has come: 13 Baktun 13 A'jau, the return of the grandparents, the return of the wise ones to the measure of time... The time has come. May the people awaken. May they arise...

We do not have much time or life left. We have only (a few) years until the Year Zero. After the Year Zero there shall be peace... We need to cultivate peace. Let us love one another. Let us defend the Earth, our Mother, and respect our Father. His sacred mandate is among us...

You and I may meet again in another dimension after the Year Zero. The Year Zero is the word of the Maya... On this day, the Sun will be hidden for a period of 60-70 hours and this is when we shall enter the period of the Sixth Sun. Then will you realize that what the Mayans speak are facts and not false preachings... The Mayan priests and astronomers know what is happening and see what shall happen in the future. This is my only message. I do not come to intimidate you. I come to say that we should love one another. Let us walk together. We are all children and we pray that our Father be with us. Thank you.[2]

Many people have offered dates for this entry into the Sixth Sun, this passage of planetary birthing. There is nothing ambivalent about the birth of a child, no questioning about whether the birth has already happened, no endless arguments about what it might look like. When a woman is pregnant, we can try and predict a due date, but we can never be sure exactly when the child will be born until the birth actually takes place.

Many feel that some kind of planetary birthing is imminent. The Mayan calendar and other prophetic systems may be offering us possible due dates. Recent scientific research may be pointing us in the same direction. But rather than fixate too heavily on dates, perhaps we might ask ourselves how we can each contribute personally to this transformational process. We are not passive observers but rather active participants in this journey. How do we use the immense power of this galactic wave to cocreate the new Earth?

chapter 4

Three Days of Darkness

The prophecy of three days of darkness, as shared by Don Alejandro Cirilo, is found in other ancient traditions as well. I had pondered often whether this prophecy was a symbolic statement of some kind, or a literal darkness involving the absence of sunlight — or perhaps something else. When we asked him to expound upon this idea during our visit with him in Guatemala, he simply shrugged his shoulders and said he didn't know. As I continued to research information about the geomagnetic reversal and its possible relationship with these three days of darkness, new insights started pouring in.

What happens when the magnetic field of the Earth collapses? Every living creature on the planet is designed to interact closely with Earth's geomagnetic field. Some species, such as migratory birds, bees, whales, and dolphins, literally have homing systems in their brains that are directly attuned to this magnetic field, much like our own GPS systems. All of us, however, depend on this geomagnetic field, not only for physical survival but also for our sense of personal identity.

Our human identity derives from our thoughts, feelings, and memories held within subtle fields around our physical bodies, which some refer to as the *etheric*, *emotional*, and *mental bodies*. When Earth's geomagnetic field collapses, however, so does our link to these subtle bodies, leading to the cessation of our physical sense mechanisms, and to a temporary dissolution of our sense of personal identity.

During this time, we literally cannot see, feel, hear, smell, touch, taste, think, or remember who we are. It is like entering into a dark slumber where the entire hardware of personal conscious-ness gets rebooted.

In our current stage of human evolution, we tend to identify with the body-mind personality because of the powerful sensory in-put constantly bombarding us, a sense of identity that reaches deep down into the subconscious mind, and even gets imprinted on our DNA. The density of this personal identity, separated from our multidimensional soul identity, is what creates the illusion of duality and separation. When the magnetic field cancels out, all of these identifications fall away, opening us up to the possibil-ity that when the system reboots, the brain could be rewired to function as an operating system for the soul rather than for the illusory ego personality!

This transformation is not so different from the journey of a cat-erpillar. There comes a stage in its life when a caterpillar dies to everything it has known before. It retreats into a cocoon and dissolves into a soup. It is a time of subjective darkness, where its physical senses cease to function and new DNA starts being produced. This DNA already exists in the caterpillar as genetic potential, but only when the caterpillar enters its cocoon does this DNA become activated, leading to the emergence of the butterfly.

Similarly, the three days of darkness may refer to a time of co-cooning, a rebooting of consciousness whereby our entire subconscious history and personal identity gets obliterated, so that something new can emerge. I believe that this event is the gateway to our future evolution as a species. As long as we are conditioned by the subconscious mind, trapped in the density of fear-based responses to life, we cannot directly access our higher selves.

14

However, as the veils of subconscious illusion drop away, our bodies begin to vibrate differently, and become capable of accessing and anchoring the frequencies of our soul. This experience is what the journey of *ascension* is about: It is the ascent of matter into spirit, and simultaneously the descent of spirit into matter. It is the awakening of our multidimensional consciousness within bodies of purified matter, with a capacity for conscious cocreation to an extent that we cannot yet imagine.

We are currently in a transitional zone, a period of preparation for this transformation of consciousness. It is a time of deep cleansing and purification. We are tired of being caterpillars, but haven't yet become butterflies. As more light comes in, more shadows get stirred up — and we discover that all the human identities and personal stories that we have carefully built up over the years suddenly start to dissolve.

Many of us seem to be going through this dissolution process now in the form of emotional upheavals, mental chaos, and physical breakdowns — intense anxiety, depression, restlessness, shock, chaos, and pain. Many are going through extreme intensity and turbulence in our relationships, sinking in a quicksand of existential meaninglessness, or feeling alone and adrift in a dark cloud of unknowing. We confront a great unknown, helpless and afraid, feeling our entire sense of identity collapse around us.

We can't focus, we forget where we left our keys, we can't remember names or faces, and wonder if we're losing our minds. Perhaps we've already done so, for all the things we cherished and enjoyed in the past don't seem so important anymore. We find ourselves wondering what we are doing on this planet. As veils of illusion fall away, *reality* seems to become more absurd by the day, leaving us with a sense of unfulfilled longing for something we cannot know because it has not yet been birthed.

Our bodies are going through a transition, too. We endure physical challenges, fatigue, aches and pains, general toxicity, and nervous breakdowns. We cannot keep up with the demands of time — and, in fact, our sense of time itself is changing. Our immune systems get overloaded as we encounter new forms of disease every day. We experience in our own bodies changes taking place in the subtle bodies of the Earth, and it is often exhausting.

On a collective level, this same dissolution of identity is manifesting as economic collapse, political unrest, social chaos, and environmental catastrophe. Nothing is certain anymore. We live in a world that has lost its balance, and seems to be spinning rapidly out of control. There doesn't seem to be a way back out.

What does this experience all mean in the bigger picture? If these are all symptoms of a transitional phase, as we are forced to release personal identities that once felt so safe and familiar, then what awaits us after we emerge from the cocoon?

chapter 5

A New Sun

When the Mayas talk about what will happen just before we enter the new world, they say there will be some days of darkness followed by a new sunrise. As Aluna Joy Yaxk'in shares:

———◦———

There is a new Sun coming up over an ocean, and there is nothing else... Just the ocean and the Sun... The Maya say they are not really sure if it is a brand-new Sun or just the energy of a new Sun, but they say a new Sun will rise. A new Sun is being manifested in spirit right now. The Ancestors are saying that this new Sun is being birthed into the world... It will take a while for this to manifest physically. When it does, we will be receiving energy in a direct way...[1]

———◦———

As with prophecies of the three days of darkness, prophecies of a second Sun are part of many other ancient traditions. How do we interpret this prediction in a way that makes sense to us in our modern age of science and reason? There are many rumors and predictions these days about super-dense planets, brown dwarf Suns, and, indeed, entire miniature solar systems blazing their way through our solar system, wreaking havoc in their path. Is this the vision that the Mayas are referring to?

I believe that prophecy is often based on ancient memories, which wisdom keepers of many traditions consult to predict future events based on cycles in the past. If so, what does this double prophecy of three days of darkness followed by the rising of a second Sun mean?

My sense is that although the Mayas may be referring to a literal event, we cannot interpret this prophecy from a third-dimensional perspective of reality. Perhaps in order to understand what this prediction means, we need first to take a journey into the deepest layers of our subconscious mind, into a matrix we might refer to as the *veil of illusion*.

Eastern spiritual traditions have much to say about the existence of certain veils of illusion, which they refer to as *maya*. A simplistic interpretation of this belief is to say that the world out there is an illusion, and that the way out of this illusion is to renounce the world. Although this response may have worked for us in simpler times, we must understand that now *the veils of illusion exist within our own consciousness*. The world out there is not the problem — our *interpretation* of this world is, based as it is on subconscious structures of programming that keep us trapped in perceptions of separation and duality.

This veil of illusion lies deep within our subconscious awareness, and is literally programmed into the matrix of our cellular DNA. The frequency of this programming keeps us trapped in a third-dimensional perception of reality, which we consider the one and only reality of existence. The belief that third-dimensional reality is the only reality is itself the illusion, and we cannot make it through the Great Shift as long as this programming remains within our cells.

Something very interesting begins to happen during the time of geomagnetic reversal. As I said earlier, as the geomagnetic field of the Earth collapses, the matrix of our personal identity begins to disintegrate. Our emotional and mental bodies are no longer tightly bound to old patterns of subconscious conditioning.

We begin to unravel the veils of illusion that keep us trapped in third-dimensional density. New potentials of genetic information become activated, which raises the frequency of the energy matrix vibrating the cells of our body, in turn helping us perceive realities beyond the narrow limits of our known physical senses. Our consciousness begins to merge with worlds and dimensions beyond third-dimensional matter. We begin to anchor the multidimensional frequencies of our soul.

All this change happens very quickly during this cocooning period, as our sensory perceptions go into hibernation during these days of darkness. Creative evolution is a quantum process that utilizes the enormous wave of in-coming cosmic energy to shape new creation. In the absence of the subconscious conditioning that has kept us trapped within the veils of illusion for eons, we make a quantum jump of evolution into a new state of biological consciousness capable of integrating the multidimensional frequencies of our soul.

Perhaps we can now interpret this prophecy of the Second Sun in a somewhat different way. Most Suns exist as part of a binary star system. Our experience in this solar system is unique in that we only perceive a single Sun. But perhaps our twin Sun has always existed on a higher octave of creation and we simply have not been able to see it yet!

Perhaps it is not that a second Sun enters our solar system during this time of the Great Shift but that our twin Sun simply becomes visible to us in this dimension, as our senses expand beyond the narrow limits imposed by linear consciousness!

This new Sun is already manifested in spirit, say the Mayas. When this new Sun manifests in the physical world, we will be receiving its energy in a direct way. We will be able to assimilate this new Sun's energy because our bodies will no longer be subject to the limitations of matter. Our bodies will be nourished directly from the energy of the new Sun.

We will learn to use the energy of this Sun to build internal technologies that directly resonate with our higher selves. We will learn to heal our bodies, create new worlds. We will travel freely through multiple dimensions of the universe. We will nourish our bodies directly from the fields of *prana* all around us. Outdated social, political, economic, and religious systems will fall away because they will no longer be needed.

As the veil of illusion dissolves, so, too, does our subconscious matrix of fear, separation, and duality. We will experience this planet as one single interconnected consciousness unifying all things within the web of life. We will discover what it means to experience Creator-Consciousness within infinite dimensions of Creation!

The Mayas remind us that the new Sun manifesting on the outside is a reflection of a new Sun being birthed within. This is the soul consciousness being birthed as we pass into the doorway of the new Earth! It is the birth of a *divine human*, serving as a steward on this beautiful blue and green planet, inspired by a constantly flowing well of creative impulse. Rather than reacting instinctively in predetermined subconscious patterns, we will respond in each moment with the full intensity of our multidimensional presence, nurturing and honoring each strand in the web of planetary life.

Whatever is real from the old Earth will remain. Experiences that feed and enrich our souls, memories of beauty and love, all of these will remain. Nothing is ever lost in evolution. Old structures are simply included and transcend to a higher octave of life. We will experience life in the same dimensions of matter, simply vibrating to a higher frequency of light. We will engage the world around us through similar personality structures, but harmonize directly to the consciousness of our souls.

This is the goal of creative evolution as we transition to the new Earth.

chapter 6

A Supramental Light

The Mayas tell us that the shift represented by Year Zero signifies the end of linear history and the beginning of a multidimensional experience of time. Our experience of linear time has to do with the way our brains are wired, and the predominance of what we could call the *thinking mind*; however, as the great Indian yogi Sri Aurobindo demonstrated more than a hundred years ago, certain levels of the mind are capable of accessing dimensions of reality far beyond the capacities of our thinking mind.

Sri Aurobindo refers to various levels of the mind, including the *higher mind*, the *illumined mind*, the *intuitive mind*, the *overmind*, and the *supermind*. I explore this concept further in my earlier books and will not go into much detail here, except to say that there are fields of consciousness associated with each of these levels of the mind, and that our perception of reality changes dramatically when accessed from different levels of the mind.

The thinking mind is designed to function within third-dimensional reality, dealing with the mechanics of survival and instinct, our physical orientation in space and time — and that's all. Our creative gifts, our capacity for joy, our perceptions of higher dimensions, the embodiment of our multidimensional self — these responses derive from our ability to access higher levels of the mind.

Sri Aurobindo and his spiritual partner, Mirra Alfassa (usually known simply as *The Mother*), spoke often about the descent of these higher levels of mind into our operational systems. Having trained themselves to merge with these higher levels of the mind, they were able to sense a new wave about to enter into human consciousness, which they referred to as the *supramental force*. They spoke of the descent of this force into the field of matter, and the resulting transformation of our species.

They recognized that in previous cycles of time, we were able to partially embody the higher levels of the mind, but could not maintain this stage as a collective consciousness, which time and again ended with a fall back to the density of physical matter. They felt, however, that in this current cycle of evolution, there was the potential to embody the highest level of unified light, what they called the *supramental light*, and in so doing to raise the frequency of matter itself into what they called *true matter*. This event would represent the birth of Creator-Consciousness within the heart of all creation!

Regarding the human species, they spoke of an evolutionary force that has been pushing us from the *animal human* stage, organized around the instinctive centers of the brain, to the *human human*, organized around thought and reason. The next step in our evolution, they said, is the *divine human*, where we would learn to connect through our hearts to the frequencies of the soul.

At this stage, our experience of reality would no longer be based on the thinking mind, designed to interpret everything through filters of duality, but rather on the intuitive mind, which perceives reality through direct knowing. Beyond this, finally, was a fourth stage of human evolution, which they called the *supramental human*. At this stage of evolution, we will walk this Earth as living embodiments of Creator-Consciousness, expressing our universal identity within bodies of *true matter*!

I believe that each time it passes through our solar system, the galactic superwave provides us an opportunity to evolve further as a species, and as a planet. It may be that the next species to collectively emerge from the upcoming geomagnetic reversal will be the divine human, an awakened species capable of experiencing the physical world through senses attuned to intuitive levels of the mind, unified with the web of planetary life.

While this appearance could well be the next step in our collective evolution, I feel that those who are ready for it will be given the opportunity to carry this evolution even further. If Sri Aurobindo is right, we will begin to incarnate as supramental beings, anchoring creative potential from dimensions beyond time and space, fully awakening within matter for the first time in the 13.8 billion years since the birth of this Universe!

chapter 7

The Golden String

We are already experiencing the first waves of this supramental light. This light has been guiding our evolution from a level of wisdom and power far beyond what is available to us within the field of duality, and it cannot be held back any more than a caterpillar can resist becoming a butterfly. From this perspective of unified light, *everything* we have ever experienced in our collective history is part of an in-built soul-directed evolutionary drive. There is no right or wrong, no good or evil.

As the Sufi Jalaluddin poet Rumi expresses so beautifully, *Out beyond ideas of wrong doing or right doing there is a field. I will meet you there*.[1]

My sense is that the actual moment of the Shift will be easy and joyous. As we disconnect from subconscious fields of separation and duality during these three days of cocooning, we will simply not be capable of going into doubt, fear, and resistance as we normally tend to do. As subconscious layers peel away, we will be able to use the incoming cosmic radiation to complete our biological transformation. Dormant genetic codes will be activated. The multidimensional presence of our higher selves will begin to incarnate through us. The butterfly will emerge!

But if the Shift itself is relatively smooth, the time immediately prior to the Shift could be quite challenging. These are the times we currently live in — what the Hopis refer to as *the day of purification* — when all our subconscious darkness is being forced to the surface to be released. Surrendering to this alchemical process is not easy, but to the extent that we can understand and trust the evolutionary forces working through us, it will help make the journey a little smoother.

There is a story of a Greek hero named Theseus and his journey through the labyrinths of Crete in order to find and slay the minotaur. In order not to lose his way through the maze, he carries with him a ball of golden string, which he unravels in the darkness so he can eventually find his way back out.

As we travel through our own maze of uncertainty and chaos in these times, perhaps we need to discover our own balls of string in order to find our way through and beyond. Perhaps this larger evolutionary perspective can guide us in the journey ahead, helping us to surrender gracefully to the energies of transformation that invite us now to enter the luminous depths of our being.

As long as we are still trapped in our current experience of duality, fear is an inevitable response to the energies of change. But, if even in the midst of this fear, we can maintain an awareness of the big picture, this awareness can be the golden string that guides us through these tumultuous times.

What if our experience of duality, and all the suffering that inevitably followed, was a necessary phase in our evolution? The higher we want to climb, the deeper we have to go. Could it be that we needed to enter into the deepest density of matter, forgetting our identity as creator gods in order to transform matter itself in our journey of remembrance?

Our addiction to personal ego has led us to the verge of socioeconomic collapse, the fulfillment of which would drastically disrupt a way of life with which we have grown quite comfortable. Our soils and oceans are dying, forests are disappearing, and millions of species are rapidly going extinct. Our own existence is only a matter of time. Unless something changes, we will either go out with a bang in some sort of catastrophic event, or slowly suffocate in our own wastes.

From a soul perspective, however, this level of global crisis is simply providing the intensity needed to propel us through an evolutionary shift. Change cannot happen as long as we are comfortable in our illusions. The evolutionary energy driving us forward is not concerned with individual lives or human timescales; it is concerned only with new possibilities of creation, the immense task of incarnating our multidimensional self within bodies of matter.

That time has come. As creator beings, we are here now to re-member who we are and to radiate our light into the world. We, as humans, are part of the nervous system of the Earth, and our destiny is to serve as cosmic conductors for a unified light so that Earth herself can evolve further. Our greatest service is simply in remembering who we are as beings of light. The more we can anchor this light through us, the easier the transformation will be for humanity and for the Earth.

On a more practical level, it seems to me that the energies of transformation are working simultaneously on many levels. Unhealthy economic and social structures need to collapse so that a new Earth can emerge. Old technologies must fail so that we can discover the power latent within our own DNA. Limited identities must die for our soul identities to be birthed. Old frequency patterns need to be shaken up so that the new Earth can be birthed. When the time is right, all this could happen very suddenly and very quickly.

The geomagnetic reversal is the key to this alchemy. Many things are likely to happen simultaneously during this time. As the veils fall away, our current social, political, and economic systems would quickly transform, coinciding with evolutionary mutations, and whatever Earth changes are needed to reorient the Earth to a higher dimensional frequency. An entirely new identity is being birthed.

The Mayas say that when we enter Year Zero, questioning whether it is truly happening will be impossible. It's like awakening from a dream. When you are dreaming, you can wonder if you're dreaming, but when you are awake, you know you are awake!

This prophecy of awakening is the golden string that guides us through the maze. If we can trust this evolutionary force and stay connected with the larger vision, we need not fear the process. Rather, we can allow ourselves to surrender to the ecstasy of birth as these powerful energies make their way through our being.

A single luminous intelligence is guiding this process, an intelligence with which we can attune and become cocreators. But we don't have to wait until the geomagnetic reversal. In the following sections of this book, I would like to explore how we can begin to access this living field of light here and now, anchoring it through our bodies to serve the evolution of the Earth. This field of light I have come to know as *Ilahinoor*.

PART II

ILAHINOOR,
A "DIVINE LIGHT"

This evening the Divine Presence, concrete and material,
was there present amongst you. I had a form
of living gold, bigger than the universe,
and I was facing a huge and massive golden door
which separated the world from the Divine.

As I looked at the door, I knew and willed,
in a single movement of consciousness,
that "the time has come," and lifting with both hands a
mighty golden hammer I struck one blow,
one single blow on the door,
and the door was shattered to pieces.

Then the supramental Light and Force and Consciousness
rushed down upon Earth in an uninterrupted flow.

The Mother (February 29, 1956)

chapter 8

Journey into Healing

I grew up in India, where knowledge of a higher world and dimensions is still held sacred. I have always been interested in healing. I remember as a teenager reading about the healing miracles of Jesus and being fascinated, especially by his assertion that "the same things I do you shall do also, and even greater, because I go unto my Father."[1] I was so excited about this idea that I went and found a priest and asked him if he could teach me how to heal like Jesus and his disciples. He smiled at my enthusiasm, but I still remember the sorrowful look in his eyes as he shook his head and said, "I'm sorry, son, but the age of miracles is over."

I was depressed for days afterward, but knew somewhere inside me that these things were still possible. I knew it had to do with our perceptions of reality. I continued reading stories of yogis and saints, shamans and healers. I spent time travelling through various ashrams in India, meditating and listening to stories of enlightened masters. Such experiences were all I wanted from my life: I wanted to get enlightened so that I could heal and serve humanity from a higher place of awareness. Nothing else mattered.

My initial enthusiasm faded somewhat when I realized that this effort was a more difficult task than I'd imagined. I didn't have the discipline to sit for long years in a cave high up in the Himalayas mastering my breath and contemplating whatever it was I was supposed to contemplate in order to get enlightened.

In my early twenties I left for the United States, and completed a B.A. in peace studies and international development. During this time, I became fascinated by Native American history and traditions. I spent a lot of time in the wilderness seeing the world through their eyes, doing vision quests and sweat lodges, learning to listen to *the spirit that moves through all things*.[2]

Ultimately I realized that it was nice to explore all these fascinating worlds, but that I needed a profession. So I enrolled in a master's program in transpersonal psychology, and eventually got licensed as a marriage and family therapist in California. I spent most of my internship years at an alternative psychiatric center in the hills of Sonoma County known as Pocket Ranch Institute.

As part of a team of like-minded people, I worked extensively with clients who had lived through every imaginable sort of trauma and abuse. I was shocked by their stories, and touched by their courage. We also worked with people going through a spiritual awakening process, and who needed a sanctuary where they could integrate new aspects of their being. Pocket Ranch was nestled in a valley surrounded by streams and forests as far as the eye could see, and contact with the wilderness became an integral part of the treatment.

Pocket Ranch was an experiment in expanding the psychiatric model to include alternative modalities. We used shamanic journeys, art therapies, dreamwork, holotropic breathwork, hypnotherapy, bodywork, primal therapies, family constellations, movement therapies — and anything else we could find to help clients discover themselves in a new way. People felt loved, honored, and listened to, and that attention was a big part of the healing.

It was a sad day for all of us when Pocket Ranch closed down. But what I learned there remains with me always. More than anything, I learned that in order to be a healer, I needed to be fully present in my heart, open to other dimensions of reality, and willing to trust fully the intuitive guidance that comes from within.

During this time I was living in a community near Mt. Shasta, a lone-standing snow-capped volcano sacred to the Native American tribes in that area. It is an interdimensional portal, and many people have experienced contact with other realities in this region, including meetings with *ascended masters* such as Babaji and St. Germain, as well as various orders of angelic beings, devas, fairies, and galactic intelligences.

Over the years, I began to develop an active relationship with these beings, and learned to communicate with them by listening through my intuitive mind. It was here, also, that I began to understand that a higher plan existed for humanity and the world as it was unfolding in these times.

As I learned to access higher dimensions of consciousness, my relationship with the ascended masters deepened. I felt especially close with Babaji, whom I experienced as an elder brother and my dearest friend. He was a guiding light on my path, inspiring me toward a planetary destiny where the divine could be fully manifest in bodies of matter. I realized that part of my work was to find certain pieces of a cosmic jigsaw puzzle and to start putting them together.

But, even more importantly, I was to embark on a journey deep into cellular consciousness in order to dissolve the veils of separation. I was told that there are doorways of light within cellular consciousness that are linked with the collective human mind, and that if I were able to find these doorways, then I could help open up this space for others.

This realization eventually led to a book, *Doorway to Eternity: A Guide to Planetary Ascension*,[3] in which I shared some of my journeys and discoveries. I remember being warned that if I wrote this book I couldn't be invisible anymore. I valued my privacy and feared that if too many people got to know me I wouldn't have a personal life left. Ultimately, I realized that the basis of this fear was my attachment to a sense of personal self, and I could ultimately let this go. A new phase of life had begun.

chapter 9

The Deeksha Movement

My journey eventually led me back to India. In late 2002, I left the United States with my partner, Grace, whom I had met at my first book signing in Mt. Shasta, and we embarked on a new adventure, travelling through ashrams and spiritual communities, meeting masters and yogis, continuing to look for pieces of a giant jigsaw puzzle that was starting to come together.

For some years we got involved in the *Deeksha movement*, originating out of Oneness University in South India. This movement was founded on the work of Sri Bhagavan and Sri Amma (different from Ammachi, the "hugging mother" of Kerala), two visionary mystics who referred to themselves as *avatars of enlightenment*. We happened to be in Oneness University during the summer of 2003, the very first time the Deekshas were publicly given. Deeksha is a transmission of divine light, which Bhagavan claimed was able to give people enlightenment. We spent several months there working with this divine energy of awakening, including learning how to transfer it to others.

I wrote a book, *Deeksha: Fire from Heaven*,[1] about this phenomenon, and for the next three or four years we travelled around the world constantly, introducing this energy to people, many of whom went on to join the Deeksha movement. We shared the vision of global awakening through the Deeksha, always in the context of what Sri Aurobindo had spoken of as *the supramental awakening*, a time when the unified consciousness of divinity becomes fully awake within the world of matter.

After some time, however, we realized that something had changed for us. Much as we respected the power of this work, and the intention of its founders, we understood that this transmission of light came from our higher selves rather than through the agency of Bhagavan and Amma, and we therefore encouraged people to experiment with tuning in to their higher selves and to share this energy with others after having received it.

This decision didn't go down well with the Movement, and we were told that people needed to be initiated directly by Oneness University if they wished to share Deeksha with others. The fee for this initiation was high, and we felt ourselves becoming increasingly reluctant to conform to the commercial and hierarchical aspects of this work, even though the Deeksha itself felt like a beautiful gift of grace.[2]

The big question in our minds was whether the divine grace that people experienced from the Deeksha was something that came exclusively from these two avatars of enlightenment, as claimed by Oneness University, or whether it was something everyone could access directly through their own higher selves. In our own experience, we had found that people were equally capable of transmitting this light by respectfully attuning to this field of higher consciousness, no matter what we chose to call it.

I deeply respected the work of Bhagavan and Amma in introducing the Deeksha field to so many people around the world in the best way they knew how. But could it be that the age of the individual avatar was ending now, and that a new age of the collective avatar had begun?

Our lives move forward in waves. Each wave comes in, and then moves back, making way for another. Between the waves is a time of questioning, a time when we get to re-examine the foundation of our being, and do the necessary work of integration before the next wave comes in from the same cosmic ocean. We allowed ourselves to enter into a space between the waves, waiting for guidance.

chapter 10

Call to Turkey

I was in Bangalore in late March 2006 when I received a phone call from my South African friend, Vivek. He was a few hours away from me, and sounded excited. "When can I see you?" he asked. I told him I didn't have much time at the moment since I was getting ready to head for Turkey in a few days, where Grace and I had been invited to do a few Deeksha seminars.

He insisted that he had to speak with me, however. He told me that he had just finished talking with his friend Rajendra, who was a seer. Vivek happened to have a copy of my book *Fire from Heaven* with him, and had shown it to Rajendra. As Rajendra held the book in his hands, he had clairvoyantly provided Vivek with various details about my life, which he proceeded to share with me over the phone.

I was intrigued. I called up Rajendra. It turned out that he was coming to Bangalore the following day, and we arranged to meet for lunch. We talked about planetary events and the journey of awakening. He repeated what Vivek had told me, but then continued, saying that although most of my work had been in the Western world so far, this focus would soon change.

He told me I would be living in the Muslim world next, and that I would be sharing an important message that would help bring peace to the world. He said I had been incarnate in Arabia during the lifetime of the prophet Mohammad and that it was time for me now to reconnect with that lineage so I could help people get in touch with a long-forgotten deeper message. He reiterated that this effort would help harmonize the major world religions.

I had spent much of my life exploring the Hindu, Buddhist, Christian, Pagan, Native American, and Shamanistic traditions. I was being called now to enter more deeply into the mystical aspects of the Muslim tradition, commonly known as Sufism.

I was still pondering all this information when Grace and I arrived in Istanbul a few days later. We had met a spiritual teacher from Istanbul a few months previously in Sicily, who had subsequently invited us to Turkey to spend some time together and do a few Deeksha events.

When we arrived in Turkey, in Spring of 2006, we were simply intending to do a couple of seminars and then return home to India. The universe, however, had a different plan. We discovered that Turkey was the home to one of the greatest Sufi masters who had ever lived, the fiery mystic poet Jelaluddin Rumi, known here simply as Mevlana. Doors continued to open, and it wasn't long before we found a seaside home in this ancient and beautiful country, amongst a warm, open-hearted, and extremely hospitable people.

chapter 11

Emergence of Ilahinoor

A couple of months after we settled in, events started unfolding very quickly. Grace was away visiting her kids in Canada. I was with a small group of people in Dalyan, a beautiful village on the Aegean coast of Turkey. Two of these women had just returned from Egypt, where they had experienced deep resonance with the pharaoh Akhenaton and his role in reviving the mystery school traditions of ancient Egypt.

As we listened to their stories, we gradually became aware of a vast energy weaving itself through the room. As we attuned to this energy, it identified itself as Ra, one of the solar deities of old Egypt. He spoke about an ancient morphogenetic field that existed for the purpose of accelerating the *ascension* process of selected initiates, many of whom had succeeded in achieving a state of ascension or *physical immortality* during various periods of Egyptian history.

The more initiates who were able to merge their physical bodies into light, the stronger this field became. This morphogenetic field was now being reactivated, said Ra. The time had come again for the doorway between the worlds to be opened and for humans to step into their divine potential. This time, however, it was not for just a few initiates. A new phase of galactic activity was beginning, and this doorway was being opened for all humanity.

As we continued to attune to these energies over the next few days, more information came through. As we worked with the energy, we were guided in the use of it, but were also told that it was important not to create any fixed rules about how it should be used. All of the people in attendance were invited to tap into the morphogenetic field directly through their own higher self, thus allowing their own guidance to teach them about the use of this divine potential.

We asked for a way to quickly connect to the vibration of this field and received the name *Ilahinoor*, which means *divine light* in Turkish and Arabic. We were told not to get too attached to any one name, as we could each spontaneously connect to this field by simply opening our hearts to it.

The Sufis have a beautiful understanding of what *divine light* means. It is not a light outside, beyond, or above, as we often associate it with our understanding of God. *Ilahinoor* refers to the light that permeates all things, surrounds all things, and connects all things. It is a unified energy field that seems to share some of the same characteristics as Sri Aurobindo's *supramental light*. This light, said Ra, was now being birthed within our hearts, and within the heart of all matter.

I found that this energy was similar in many ways to what I had experienced when swimming with humpback whales in Hawaii, when I had felt my body losing its sense of physical boundaries, and merging with Earth, Sky, and beyond. The energy was powerful and entered deeply into the physical body. It was warm and fluid, and felt very nourishing.

The expansion I had felt in my encounter with the mother humpback whale was stimulated by waves of light I had felt beaming in through an area in the back of the head. This area of the brain represented a link to *spherical consciousness*, they had told me, a multidimensional experience of reality that was now being birthed within the human species. The whales were physiologically designed to maintain this consciousness at all times, and now the time had come for humans to embody this consciousness as well.

As we experienced the Ilahinoor energies in Dalyan, we were now instructed to work with these same points in the back of the head. We were told that this place was related to an area of the old brain through which we could rewrite our genetic codes, which was the potential of the Ilahinoor work. We were instructed to place one hand on the back of the head and the other hand on the forehead, creating a bridge through which Ilahinoor could enter subconscious realms of awareness and do whatever clearing and healing was necessary.

We experimented with holding these points while inviting Ilahinoor to come through and asking the whales to link in interdimensionally. People began to experience amazing ex-pansions of consciousness, just like I had back in Hawaii while swimming with the humpbacks.

chapter 12

A Bridge
to the Subconscious

Over the next few weeks, I continued doing the Ilahinoor work with other groups. As people began sharing their experiences, certain common patterns began to emerge. I realized that somehow bridges were being created among the subconscious, conscious, and superconscious aspects of the self.

There is a powerful ancient Hawaiian healing tradition known as Huna. The keepers of this tradition, the Kahunas, believe that we are a composite of three selves, the *high self*, the *middle self*, and the *low self*, corresponding to the superconscious, conscious, and subconscious aspects of the mind. They believe that the *middle self* cannot directly access the higher planes of existence. There is a link, however, between the *low self* and the *high self*, and by developing a relationship with the subconscious mind, we can access these superconscious aspects of our being.

These points in the back of the head were an energetic access into the limbic system, and specifically the *amygdala*. This primitive part of the brain is linked to subconscious aspects of the mind and is where we carry imprints of fear, trauma, separation, and duality. These subconscious tendencies are so instinctive and so deep-seated that even when we are able to develop greater awareness of these patterns, changing them is not easy.

The forehead, meanwhile, is an access point to the third eye, crown chakra, and axiatonal lines, which are related to the higher frequencies of the superconscious mind. Because these two areas of the brain are energetically linked together through the Ila-hinoor field, a bridge may be created between the superconscious and subconscious aspects of the mind, releasing deep-seated patterns of conditioning and trauma, and embodying more of our divinity.

My experiences with this field were very similar to what we had experienced earlier with Deeksha. As we experimented, we began to realize that these two streams of evolutionary energy were very complementary in their purposes — although quite different as well.

Like the Deeksha, Ilahinoor represents a cosmic evolutionary energy, whose purpose is to prepare us for the great awakening. Unlike the Deeksha, Ilahinoor can be accessed directly from the Cosmic Source, without using intermediaries.

Over the next few months, as a system evolved to share this new energy, people began to provide enthusiastic feedback about the effectiveness of Ilahinoor in their lives. People found themselves going into profound states of cosmic union that were expanded as well as embodied. Many reported a clearing of deep-seated addictions and emotional pain. Others even reported physical healings, as the divine energies worked with subconscious realms to dissolve karmic blocks and childhood patterns.

Many people felt the Ilahinoor energy not only in the upper chakras but also in the solar plexus, the center for personal will and power. Experimenting with holding a specific intention while receiving these energies creates a fusion of personal will with divine will, allowing for a deeper manifestation of divinity in whatever areas of life we wish to focus on.

For most of us, the fears and conditioning held within our subconscious minds block the conscious manifestation of our divine potential. As we worked with these areas of the old brain, using the power of divine light, we learned to harmonize superconscious intention with subconscious potential in order to consciously create desired realities.

All this work is very much in its experimental stages. The possibilities are endless. There are so many different expressions of divine energy, each of which may have specific functions, but I see them all as braiding together into a single evolutionary focus.

Having worked actively as a transpersonal psychotherapist for many years, I am excited about the potential of Ilahinoor for achieving profound emotional healing, as well as for more deeply integrating divine light into the physical body. Many therapists are starting to integrate this effort into their practice with clients, as are healers, medical doctors, addiction therapists, and ordinary people looking for deeper meaning in their lives. It seems to me that this practice is a way of accelerating the supramental manifestation of unified consciousness within the cellular body, in the tradition of Sri Aurobindo and the Mother.

It was not surprising to discover the link between these two traditions. The Mother has said that she was Queen Tiyi, mother of the Pharaoh Akhenaton; meanwhile, Grace feels that Sri Aurobindo was the reincarnation of Akhenaton himself!

The morphogenetic field of Ilahinoor is ancient and strong. Like Deeksha, it includes the potential for healing the body, mind, heart, and soul to an unprecedented extent by restructuring DNA in accordance with a divine blueprint. Our bodies are multidimensional temples of God, simply waiting to be transformed into vehicles for supramental light.

I have been encouraging people who have been initiated into the Ilahinoor light to experiment with initiating others. The power of this light grows with the act of sharing. It is time to move beyond hierarchies and human structures. The initiation comes not from a person or an organization but from a Cosmic Source. Each candle can directly light another from a single cosmic flame.

It is my hope that we will do this work wisely and well, giving and receiving freely from the heart, awakening each other to the destiny that awaits us collectively. Sri Aurobindo spoke of the birthing of a new species of humanity, referring to this event as the *supramental awakening*. The full awakening may take some time yet. Perhaps Ilahinoor is another wave of cosmic light moving through humanity today to prepare our bodies for this awakening.

chapter 13

Return to Egypt

In February 2008, Grace and I, along with many others from around the world, found ourselves in Egypt. Although it was my first visit there, it felt in many ways like we were returning to an ancient homeland. We had come to reconnect with the spiritual energies of this ancient world, and to explore the mysterious connection with Akhenaton that we had each felt so strongly. We also wished to touch the mystical sources of Ilahinoor, and to explore the initiatory possibilities of this morphogenetic field.

We started our trip at Gouda Fayed's *Sphinx Guest House*, overlooking the magnificent Giza Plateau, directly across from the Sphinx. Beyond this structure were the three pyramids, Khufu, Khefra, and Menkaura, majestic in their size and beauty, powerful in their ancient presence.

We then began a long journey down the Nile, beginning with the temple of Philae in Aswan, and travelling through Abu Simbel, Komombo, Edfu, Luxor, Karnak, Hatshepsut, Dendera, Abydos, and, finally, to Tel el Amarna, the City of the Horizon built by Akhenaton, before returning once again to Giza.

Our guide, Mohammed Fayed, was a professor of archaeology at the Cairo University with a unique gift for presenting us with the archaeological as well as spiritual significance of the sites we explored. He explained that the temples we were visiting represented a network of chakras. Our journey down the Nile thus symbolized the awakening of Kundalini within our own bodies as well as along the Nile, beginning with the root chakra at Philae and culminating with the crown chakra at the Great Pyramid, to which we returned for a final ceremony.

Approximately 12,000 years ago, a great cataclysm took place. In the wake of a galactic superwave, and the resulting sequence of events, the magnetic poles of the Earth got flipped around. This occurrence happened simultaneously with an event known as *crustal plate displacement*, by which the outer crust of the Earth, including seas and continents, disconnected from the inner core of the Earth and began to slip. The resulting concussion caused continents to shift, and sent most of Atlantis to the bottom of the sea.

The collapse and realignment of the magnetic fields was like pressing a reset button in Earth's evolution, and brought about a massive shift of consciousness. For those who were prepared for this event, a tremendous burst of Kundalini flowed through their bodies, dissolving the sense of separate ego identity held within the physical personality. Simultaneously, new levels of soul awareness were brought into embodiment, culminating in the transformation of the physical body into a body of light. A select few were able to pass through these gates of ascension into higher dimensional worlds.

Those who were not prepared for this transformation went beneath the waves, or sailed off to far-flung regions of the Earth to begin life anew. The process of evolution started again through slow incarnational cycles, and we have arrived once more as a species at the threshold of the *divine human*. Those of us who remained behind in the previous cycle are now preparing to make another attempt to merge our bodies into light.

Egypt was one of the destinations of surviving Atlanteans. The pharaohs and priesthood of ancient Egypt clearly remembered the events of 12,000 years previous, and were attempting — through their initiatory paths and mummification rites — to recreate the possibility of ascension for an elite few. The gateway to the higher dimensions was still open to them, a dimension which they referred to as the *Halls of Amenti*. Their entire religion was based on their knowledge and access to these Halls of Amenti, an akashic library where the deeper understandings of divine evolution and cycles of time are forever preserved.

The spiritual psychology of the ancient Egyptians reflected a deep understanding of cosmic forces. The physical body was known to them as the *khat*. The physical personality, including all the etheric, mental, and emotional imprints of a given incarnation, was called the *ka*. The luminous astral body was the *akh*, which when refined through long spiritual training, enabled an initiate to consciously travel between dimensions, and to the Halls of Amenti. The *ba* was the soul, eternal and undying. And, finally, there were the *neters*.

The neters were the gods and goddesses of the Egyptian pantheon, divine personalities familiar to us as Thoth, Ra, Osiris, Isis, Horus, Set, Maat, Nut, Geb, Hathor, Sekhmet, Anubis, and so on. Some speak of twenty-two primary neters, each representing an aspect of divine wholeness.

One of the foundational myths of ancient Egypt is the story of Osiris and Isis, and their betrayal by Set, who kills and dismembers Osiris, casting his body to the four winds. Isis, using her magical arts, goes on a quest for the missing pieces, finally putting most of him back together and breathing life into him for a brief moment. Through divine conception, Horus is born, and avenges the death of his father by killing Set.

Translations of the *Egyptian Book of the Dead*, inscribed hieroglyphically along some of the tombs in the Valley of the Kings, indicate that this story could have been a real-life drama that took place during the last days of Atlantis. It is even possible that all the neters had their origins in actual living beings during the early migrations from Atlantis, and later became deified. Like the Greek and Hindu gods, the neters of ancient Egypt embody a vast archetypal terrain.

As we connected with the energies of these neters by journeying through the sacred temples dedicated to them, we soon began to realize that these powers were neither good nor bad in themselves. Each of these neters exists within each one of us, and each of them could have both a dark face and a light face. They are simply reflections of archetypal qualities within our own psyches, and our human task is to grow in love, wisdom, and power as we integrate these qualities within.

A touching example was the story that Mohammed shared with us as we visited Sekhmet's healing room in Karnak. Like the Hindu goddess Kali, Sekhmet presents two distinct faces. During a time when mankind had degenerated into great evil, the creator gods chose the lion-headed goddess Sekhmet to obliterate the human race. The dark face of Sekhmet was revealed as she went about her terrible work of destruction.

Having accomplished her task, she remained in a state of fierce madness, and Osiris was chosen to find a way to bring her back to sanity. Turning himself into a playful monkey, Osiris slowly gained her trust and, finally revealing his true form, accompanied her back to the realm of the gods, where she eventually learned to excel in the arts of healing. Thus it happened that destruction and healing are both aspects of Sekhmet. Like their counterparts on Earth, each of the neters may have corresponding dual aspects.

chapter 14

The Mystery of Akhenaton

As we travelled, we also began to understand a little more about the controversial pharaoh Akhenaton. As he opened himself to the divine archetype of Aton, he experienced the unity of all things as reflected in the symbol of the solar disk. As a consequence, he revived the long-forgotten mystery school traditions that had provided initiates with direct access to their divine mastery.

Yet, as powerful as his experience of cosmic consciousness may have been, and though sincere in his desire to share this experience with his people through the worship of the solar disk, Aton made the mistake of denying the reality of the other neters and dismantling the old religion that was dedicated to serving them. Whether it was Akhenaton himself who was responsible for this mistake — or those who followed him — the beautiful insight of the One existing *within* the Many was distorted into a struggle of the One *against* the Many. This mistake was costly, creating a massive schism within the priesthood, and eventually bringing about the demise of ancient Egypt.

Many historians believe that Moses was a contemporary of Akhenaton, possibly his brother, Akhmoses; others believe that he may, indeed, have been Akhenaton himself and that his exodus from Egypt was what led to the demise of Tel el Amarna. It is very probable that the monotheistic beliefs of the Hebrews, which later gave rise to Christianity and Islam, are rooted in the Aton worship instituted by Akhenaton.

Although this concept of a single unifying reality may have been an important new awareness for those times, an unfortunate result of dismantling the old gods during the time of Akhenaton was the suppression of the feminine aspects of divinity. The Egyptian pantheon had been equally balanced between the masculine and the feminine. Goddesses like Isis, Sekhmet, Hathor, Maat, and Nepthys were equal in power to gods like Osiris, Horus, Thoth, Ra, and Ptah.

Raising Aton above the rest of the Egyptian pantheon established a patriarchial hierarchy in which a male God ruled supreme. This patriarchial hierarchy eventually led to a worldview in which God no longer existed within Creation, but rather was perceived as distant and separate from the natural forces of life. A dualistic understanding of religion and reality was thus established within the collective consciousness of humanity.

Many people experience Ilahinoor as a feminine energy, focused within the body, and connected to the life-giving roots of Mother Earth, and as a return to the mystical heart of life, where all things are connected in oneness. As the morphogenetic field of Ilahinoor continues to become stronger, could this strengthening help heal the masculine-feminine split ingrained so deeply within the human psyche?

When this healing happens and the feminine face of God is equally honored, could this change also mend the splits between the world's monotheistic religions? And when God is experienced as being alive within all Creation, could this awareness help heal the splits between heart and mind, body and spirit, heaven and Earth, which have kept us from experiencing this Divine Presence directly within our own lives?

As our group in Egypt visited the city of Tel el Amarna that Akhenaton had built, I experienced a momentary overlighting of his presence through my body. Simultaneously standing over a beautiful temple city at the height of Akhenaton's reign and looking out over a vast expanse of desert sand where nothing now remains, I recognized that it was time for all truths to come together. *The many are returning to the one, even as the one is reflected in the many.* There was a sense that all was as it should be, and that the vision that had awakened and that was later embodied through Sri Aurobindo would soon be realized.

chapter 15

Darkness into Light

What happens during the upcoming geomagnetic reversal on Earth will determine our future evolution as a species. During my trip to Egypt, I began to realize that there may be a relationship between the twenty-two primary neters and the twenty-two sets of chromosomes that we carry in our DNA; and perhaps it wasn't such a coincidence that there were twenty-two members in our little group!

In integrating these neters within our own psyches, are we somehow activating deeper levels of DNA potential? Scientists have only been able to uncode about 3% of the DNA proteins. The rest of it is considered *junk*. Could this junk DNA somehow carry the potential for our evolution into the *divine human*? And could a right understanding of the neters, coded within the morphogenetic field represented by Ilahinoor, be a means of activating this process?

If this were the case, I realized that one final piece needed to be finished before our work in Egypt was complete — and that was to embrace a quality of the divine that most of us feel a bit uncomfortable with, the neter represented by the "evil" god *Set*.

I began to realize that, as a god of power and magic, Set plays a necessary role in our lives, and carries great constructive potential. Only when divorced from love and wisdom does his power become dangerous, turning to violence, manipulation, hatred, aggression, and greed.

As I sat in my room directly across from the Giza plateau, I asked the Sphinx to be my guide through the Halls of Amenti, where I could come before Set and hear what he had to say. I felt a rush of energy moving through my body, and soon felt Set's words resonating inside me.

———◦———

Not many dare to come to these sacred halls where you now stand, and I will speak with you as you desire. Be alert however. You may not be ready to hear what I have to say. And you may break under the weight of my words. Yet you have come and I see you standing fearless in your kha, and I will continue to speak until we are complete.

There is a power that has lain dormant for much of humanity. It is the power of creation. It is the power of magic. I, too, am a guardian of this magic. It is the magic of power, the power to create and the power to destroy.

This power is neither good nor evil. Do not look to me through eyes jaded by human concepts. I am brother to Osiris. I represent an elemental power of the Earth just as he represents an elemental power of the stars.

The story you have heard represents the resurrection of the soul from its long sleep within Earthly dimensions. Isis is the mother of light and priestess of a divine magic, and I revere her as no other. Yet the great drama had to be played out so that the chains of matter could be broken, and this drama will continue to be played out in your world until it is complete.

Look to me inside you even as you look to Isis, Osiris, and the others from Amenti. You are not playing in puddles of human existence anymore. The spell of death hangs over you and you know it not. You weave your lives of pathetic misery and you call this aliveness. Is this what you choose to manifest with your god-given powers?

The death I deal is a prelude to resurrection. The power I give must be earned through your dedication and commitment to humanity.

Many there have been who failed in themselves to integrate these elemental powers. And the blame has always fallen on me.

Humans have learned to fear me as evil. Yet evil is only a judgment that is made when the mirror can no longer recognize its wholeness, and breaks into tiny pieces of itself. Besides, know that the gods themselves are evolving. You are the mirrors through which we, too must evolve.

There is a final gateway upon your path, a final test of courage and commitment. This is to face your own fears of the dark power, which has nothing to do with me. It is to face your own fragmentation of the soul as you descend through the veils.

The dark power is the magic of the Earth, just as the light power is the magic of the stars. In the hands of Isis, fueled by the passion of her love for Osiris, a doorway to new worlds of creation was opened. You are going through this same passage now as you prepare for the planetary shift you write about. But it means that you learn to distinguish between false power, which is abusive, and true power, which is creative. It means that you allow yourself to feel the full power of creation flowing through the dark forgotten places of your being, a power held within the cells of matter, a power deep within the DNA of your divine construction.

Any of the divine powers acting on their own ultimately create chaos. But when the twenty-two powers of creation come together in wholeness, the passage between worlds is opened up.

I share with you an understanding, on behalf of all of us at Amenti. These twenty-two powers of creation together are a morphogenetic field of new creation. Know that the Ilahinoor work you are reclaiming during this time can harmonize and in-tegrate these powers within your psyche and within your DNA, for it comes not from Ra alone but from all the neters of Amenti. Remember this as you work with this continually evolving mor-phogenetic field.

Go now in peace.

This conversation with Set was a powerful reminder that cre-ation and destruction are not separate. It is very possible that as we enter the period of *purification* preceding the Shift, things will start getting somewhat chaotic. If the timing of this event has anything to do with the ending of the Mayan calendar, we are already entering this time of chaos, which Set has referred to as the *final gateway*, and Sri Aurobindo as the *supramental catastrophe*.

Sri Aurobindo and the Mother felt from their own experiences that the Supramental Earth already exists in a different dimen-sion than our own; perhaps we might call this the Fifth Dimension or the Sixth Dimension. Perhaps this is where the Halls of Amenti exist. They felt that all that was needed to bring this dimension into planetary experience was to link to the galactic conscious-ness within ourselves and let it become externalized.

Lead us, Great Spirit, from the unreal to the real, from darkness to light, from death to immortality. Lead us through the door-ways of galactic consciousness so that we may create a heaven on Earth.

PART III

PRACTICE
GUIDELINES

Until one is committed, there is hesitancy,
the chance to draw back, always ineffectiveness.
Concerning all acts of initiative and creation,
there is one elementary truth
the ignorance of which kills countless ideas
and splendid plans:
That the moment one definitely commits oneself,
then Providence moves too.
All sorts of things occur to help one that would
never otherwise have occurred.
A whole stream of events issues from the decision,
raising in one's favor all manner of unforeseen incidents,
meetings and material assistance which no
man could have dreamed would have come his way.
Whatever you can do or dream you can, begin it.
Boldness has genius, power and magic in it.
Begin it now.

— Johan Wolfgang von Goethe

chapter 16

Experiments
with Ilahinoor

Ilahinoor is a cosmic evolutionary energy. Like many other healing systems sweeping the planet today, including Reiki, Amanae, Deeksha, Matrix Energetics, Pranic Healing, Quantum Touch, Theta Healing, Reconnection, and so many others, the purpose of Ilahinoor healing is to help humanity awaken to its infinite potential.

Although LaViolette's galactic superwave, traveling close to the speed of light, has not yet reached us in our solar system, we may be in the preparatory phases for it. Our bodies, hearts, and minds are being gradually rewired in anticipation of the sudden evolutionary energies that may be shortly coming our way.

The purpose of these cosmic pulses, by whatever name we refer to them, is to raise the molecular frequencies of all matter in our solar system, a process that some refer to as Ascension. This event also correlates to a shift of consciousness being experienced on all planets in our solar system, including, of course, here on Earth.

One function of these new frequencies in humans is that they activate dormant functions within our nervous systems and brains, resulting in the experience of multidimensional consciousness. Simultaneously, these frequencies activate new codes within our DNA, which begins a process of transformation within the human species.

The Ilahinoor work is a process of integrating these cosmic evolutionary energies for the purpose of awakening. Evolution has a way of proceeding very gradually for long periods of time, and then suddenly taking a quantum leap. We are now evolving from a species focused on physical survival, competitiveness, and aggression to a species that can integrate the frequencies of soul directly within the brain and nervous system.

As I discussed earlier, Sri Aurobindo referred to this emerging species as the *divine human*. Rather than being trapped in a linear dimension of the time-space continuum, we will ultimately experience ourselves as multidimensional beings able to move around in time and space at will, unfettered by perceived limitations of disease, aging, and death.

For many years, I have felt that our spiritual work was about embodying this divine consciousness within bodies of matter. As I continued using Ilahinoor with groups all over Turkey, Europe, and India, thousands of people reported that they were experiencing, often for the very first time in their lives, the ability to maintain expanded states of consciousness while being very consciously present in their physical bodies.

While first working with the Ilahinoor energy, I was somewhat cautious, reluctant to share this experience with too many people; likewise, I was discouraging people from sharing these energies with the larger public without first monitoring the results with themselves and one or two others. As people began to share experiences, we were all amazed by the power and potential of this work. Interestingly, people who had only recently experienced the energies were having the same kinds of results as those who had been working with these energies for a long time.

We began to realize that we were tapping into a vast and powerful morphogenetic field, which we could access not just in deep states of meditation but in the crucible of our daily lives. We began to recognize that anyone could access as well as transmit this energy to others.

chapter 17

The Basic Treatment

As we continued experimenting with these energies, we would have people working in pairs, usually sitting in chairs facing each other. We would first show people where these points were located. A sensitive area just above the occipital ridge serves as a gateway to the old brain, and seems to be where a lot of our subconscious energies can be accessed. We called these the *Ilahinoor points*.

In order to locate these points, we would first have people find the gall bladder 20 acupuncture points along the occipital ridge in the back of the head, right at the base of the skull where it meets the back of the neck. Then, about 2 or 3 cm up from there, and on a plane extending to the middle of the ears, they would find two *hollows*, a sensitive or sore spot for most people.

We would start by gazing into each other's eyes for a couple minutes to make a soul contact. The eyes are windows to the soul, and many people find that this kind of unconditional gazing quickly brings them into a sense of shared soul presence. The giver would then hold the Ilahinoor points on the receiver with one hand, while covering the receiver's forehead and crown with the other hand. We called this the *Ilahinoor bridge*.

Both people would connect with their higher selves, tune into the Ilahinoor field, and invite the energy to come through, while holding whatever intention they wished to manifest in accordance with their highest good. If they wished to invite their own masters, teachers, angels, or guides — or any aspect of the divine they felt a resonance with — they could do that as well.

The giver would hold the points for a few minutes, or as long as they felt intuitively guided, and then the receiver would take a few minutes to stay in this receptive silence. Afterwards, they would reverse places, and the receiver would become the giver. Interestingly, many said they felt more intense energies channeling through them while *giving* an Ilahinoor treatment than while *receiving* one.

As the work evolved, we were guided to add other hand positions. After holding the Ilahinoor bridge for a few minutes, the hand held over the forehead would move down to the heart chakra in the center of the chest, creating a contact between the old brain and the heart. This hand could optionally move down next to just below the sternum to make a contact between the old brain and the solar plexus.

After this step, with one hand extended palm upward connecting with cosmic light, the giver would point the extended *pinkie* (little finger) of the other hand directly into the third eye, a short distance away from the physical body, activating the pineal gland. The little finger represents the element of fire, since the heart meridian and small intestine meridian both run through this finger. The heart meridian represents the fire of spirit, or *shen*, while the small intestine represents the fire of digestion, or *chi*. Using the little finger like a laser, we would let ourselves become channels for cosmic light to energize the Kundalini fires within the third eye.

Once this transmission felt complete, the hand that was facing upward would extend down toward the Earth, this time with the intention of bringing up the Earth light and channeling it into the third eye using the same fire finger. The balance of cosmic light and Earth light is important. One is electrical in nature, the other magnetic. Feel intuitively what is needed at the time and continue channeling these energies until it feels complete. When we feel stressed and overwhelmed, we often need the energies of Mother Earth to balance us. At other times, we may need to connect with the Cosmic Source to find our inspiration and joy.

We would end with the *tube of light* to balance and ground the energies. The giver reaches up above the receiver's head to connect with the edges of an etheric tube extending vertically down through the aura of the receiver. This tube goes all the way up to the Cosmic Source and then extends all the way down to the center of the Earth.

After reaching up as high as we can to make a connection with the Cosmic Source, we slowly bring our hands down, feeling the energy balancing out through all the chakras above, within, and below the physical body, until it is anchored in the very heart of the Earth — like dropping an anchor from a boat. Once the Ilahinoor energies are anchored through the person and deep within the Earth, the winds may come and the tides may roll but the person's energy remains balanced and stable.

We would then end with the *Holographic Merkaba*, as described in the following chapter.

For those who would like to experiment with the Ilahinoor work, a summary of the Basic Treatment follows:

One on one - Basic Treatment

1. Create a sacred space with appropriate music, if desired. Many find that music incorporating the sounds of whales and dolphins can be especially powerful. Find a partner and choose who goes first. Make a prayer or invocation if you wish. The following steps are described from the perspective of the giver.

2. Holding hands, and with chairs facing each other, create a *soul merge* by gazing into each other's eyes. Meanwhile, attune to the Ilahinoor field in whatever way works for you. You may want to repeat the word *Ilahinoor* to yourself, or visualize the energy as a golden rain gently flowing in through the crown. Invoke your higher self and your spiritual guides, if you wish. Just intending to make the connection is usually enough. When you feel the energy flowing through you, begin the transmission.

   Some people may feel initially uncomfortable with direct eye contact, in which case you may want either to skip this step or simply hold hands together with eyes closed.

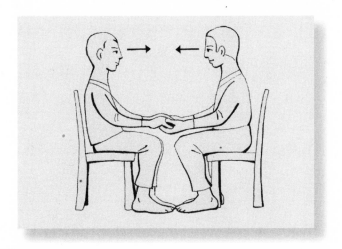

3. Create the *Ilahinoor bridge* by holding one hand over the *Ilahinoor points* in the back of the head, and the other hand over the forehead and crown. Hold the head lightly, allowing room for whatever shaking or movements want to happen.

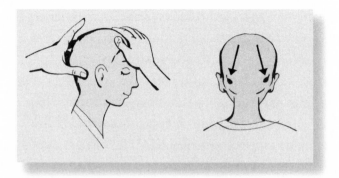

4. Make a *heart activation* by keeping one hand on the *Ilahinoor points* at the back of the head, while bringing the other hand down to the *heart chakra*.

You may optionally continue moving from heart chakra to solar plexus with one hand, while making contact with the Ilahinoor points with the other.

5. With the palm of one hand facing up toward the Cosmic Source, use the *pinkie* (little finger) of the other hand as if it were a laser beam to channel this cosmic energy into the third eye, slightly away from the body. Keep your eyes open at this point so that your finger maintains its focus.

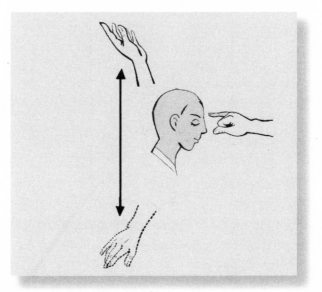

6. With the pinkie remaining in position, move the other hand down, facing the Earth. Begin channeling Earth energy up into the third eye.

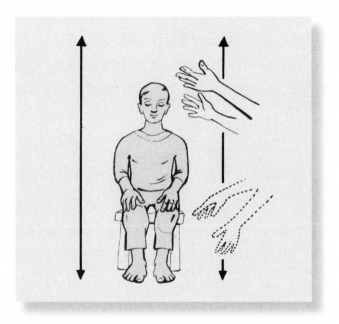

7. End with the *tube of light*. Reaching up with both hands as
    high as you can above the person's head to connect with
    their higher self, or Source, sense a tube of light extend-
    ing about one meter or more in diameter out from their
    body. This tube extends all the way up to the cosmos and
    all the way down to the center of the Earth, including all
    the chakras between. Starting with the Source, slowly move
    your hands down along the edges of this tube of light until
    you anchor the energy into the very center of the Earth.

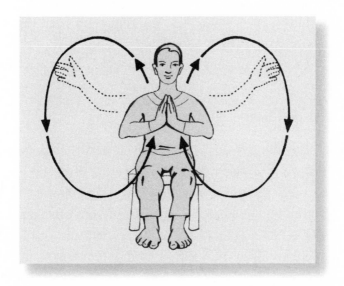

8. *Holographic Merkaba.* Holding your hands palms together over your own heart, feel yourself attuning to the heart chakra of the receiver. When the moment feels right, take a deep breath, then quickly extend your hands out and around as you expel your breath, activating the *merkaba* of the receiver. Do this gesture twice: once to activate the spin in one direction, and again to activate the spin in the other direction.

This is the basic Ilahinoor treatment. When you are giving, remember that you are simply serving as a channel for the energy, which has its own intelligence. You are not *doing* anything or trying to *make* anything happen. Ilahinoor will flow through you and go where it is needed. The more you relax, the more you will find your hands being guided. Follow your intuitive sense of how long they need to remain in each position.

Following the transmission, allow some time to integrate the energy before swapping roles and starting again from the beginning.

Ending with a hug is always nice. You may both want to rest afterwards. Lying down for a few minutes, allowing your breath to become deep, slow, and rhythmic, can help integrate your experience of the energy. Drink plenty of water following a transmission.

Basic Self-Treatment

You may also do this treatment on yourself. Simply close your eyes to establish your connection with the Ilahinoor field, and then use the same hand positions on yourself. You may find it easier to place your entire hand around the back of your head instead of awkwardly bending your wrists trying to hold the points. Once you have worked with the Ilahinoor bridge for some time, simply having the intention to connect with the Ilahinoor field is often enough to get the energy flowing.

It helps to lie down comfortably, perhaps with relaxing music, and give yourself time to fully receive this energy. Breathe deeply and rhythmically. A good time to practice Ilahinoor on yourself is immediately upon awakening, while you are still halfway in the dream worlds of the subconscious mind. You can also practice the Ilahinoor bridge at the first signs of physical stress or emotional distress during the day.

Distance Transmission

Once you are familiar with the Ilahinoor field, you can simply visualize a person or focus on their picture to send them a transmission. Use your hands in a blessing position, if that feels right. If the person is receiving a long-distance session at a predetermined time, he or she can continue relaxing for a while after the transmission is over in order to integrate the energy further. The transmission can also be conducted over the phone.

Distance transmissions can be especially powerful when you have an entire group of people focusing their energies toward a person, place, or situation. In seminars, we often have people sit in a circle and call upon various individuals in need of healing to take their place in the center. This transmission may include people who are physically present in the circle, or people whom we would invite in energetically.

We would then extend our palms out to send an Ilahinoor transmission for physical or emotional healing, or whatever else is needed. This practice can be done with individuals or entire communities or countries, for instance, if a part of the world is experiencing a natural disaster or human conflict. We can work with world leaders and specific situations; or, we can simply invite the entire planet with all her ecosystems to receive the cosmic light in her journey of awakening.

Ideally, it is helpful to transmit Ilahinoor from a place of unconditional love and acceptance, asking simply for the highest good of the person, situation, or planet. This attitude is especially important when we wish for the healing of a loved one who is sick or dying. We naturally wish to pray for a recovery, but we must not get overly attached to a particular outcome.

It may be, for instance, that someone is choosing to use an illness in order to leave the body and move on to another dimension of experience, in which case it would not be right to hold him or her back. If the soul is choosing to leave, then the transmission can serve as a beautiful gift of light to help open up the way. So whatever intention we seek, it is always good to ask the receiver's higher self to use the healing for whatever serves his or her highest good.

As we continued to experiment, additional treatment patterns were created, as described later in this book. But first, I would like to explore a light technology that I refer to as the *Holographic Merkaba*.

chapter 18

The Holographic Merkaba

I have always felt that we are capable of far more than we know. During the years I lived in Mt. Shasta, California, I had become deeply interested in *ascension*, a process of merging the physical body with the light body as a means of experiencing multidimensional consciousness in physical form. I never thought it was really possible until the day, while hiking in the mountains, I met one of these ascended masters. After telling me certain things about my past and future, he promptly dematerialized, initiating me on a journey that continues today.

The journey has taken me through various means of accessing divine light, such as *deeksha* and *Ilahinoor*. It took me into a deeper understanding of what is happening on the planet and within our galaxy, as I have outlined in previous chapters. And, in January 2009, it led me to an ancient practice of rejuvenation known as *kayakalpa*, and to an ayurvedic doctor in India, Dr. Raviraj Kadle, who has made it his mission to revive this ancient practice.

Yogic texts are filled with examples of yogis in olden times who lived up in their caves and Himalayan mountaintops. They lived for hundreds, sometimes thousands, of years in relative seclusion, working on purifying their subtle bodies, and transforming their physical bodies into light. They were known as *siddha masters*, or *adepts*. They would come down from their caves every few decades in order to undergo a specific rejuvenation process under the supervision of a specialized ayurvedic practitioner, and then go back up to continue what they were doing.

This kayakalpa process would typically last nine months and was done in near-complete darkness. After an initial cleansing, various herbs and a form of specially processed powdered gold ash would be ingested on a daily basis, which would allow the pineal gland to open. This opening would activate the rejuvenative powers of the endocrine system so as to effectively reverse the aging process.

I decided to contact Dr. Kadle, and start off with an introductory twenty-one-day program. During this time I remained inside a tiny room in near-complete darkness, cleansing, meditating, and ingesting the herbs and gold ash provided by Dr. Kadle. The gold activated a deep sensitivity to the inner light, which was sometimes so strong as to be almost blinding.

One day I had the vision of an intricate spherical design in front of my eyes, similar to a three-dimensional *flower of life*. I had, for many years, been practicing Drunvalo Melchizedek's *Merkaba meditation* for activating the light body, and this experience felt somehow related. A couple days later, I saw this bright sphere again, but this time it was embedded with *curled up dimensions* that would be impossible for me to describe in ordinary language. I realized I was seeing the geometries for a new layer of my light body.

The *Merkaba* refers to a field of higher-dimensional geometries that connect the physical body with the higher bodies. The linguistic origins of this term go back to ancient Egypt. *Ka* represents a luminous counterpart of the physical body, whose function was to feed and maintain the physical form in perfect health. *Ba* represents the soul. Thus, the *Merkaba* represents the *merging* of the *ka* with the *ba*, a geometrical matrix that unifies the flow of energies between the physical body and the light body.

After attuning to the image of this geometrical structure, I experimented with using my breath to activate this Merkaba around my body, and was shown some simple techniques to lock this

Merkaba into place. I also experimented with extending this Merkaba outward in all directions through the use of Drunvalo's expelling breath.

I noticed that whenever I practiced this meditation, unusually strong winds would come up, often blowing through the entire night. By somehow activating and linking my own Merkaba to the collective Merkaba fields, a cleansing process was being initiated that extended out to the surrounding land.

At this point, the meditation I was doing was similar to Drunvalo's system except that the geometry of the Merkaba was different. As I continued to practice this meditation, I realized that my inner self could activate this new Merkaba field very quickly if I first called in the Ilahinoor energy and anchored it through my body.

This practice evolved into what I call the *Holographic Merkaba*. After anchoring the Ilahinoor energies, I would place my hands in prayer position over my heart chakra, take a deep breath, and then rapidly move my hands above and around my body while expelling my breath quickly and forcefully with a popping sound, returning to the heart from below in the same rapid movement. It was like tracing an apple or torroidal shape out into the aura, starting and ending in the heart. I would perform this action twice for each stage of expansion as I gradually linked further and further out into the cosmos.

I took another group to Egypt shortly after the end of my kayakalpa experience. At one point, after visiting one of the temples, we felt the presence of ancient deities guiding us into doing the Holographic Merkaba as a group, progressively linking our personal energy fields with collective and planetary fields through the activation of this Holographic Merkaba.

Shortly after this experience, I was teaching a seminar in Germany, where one of the course participants shared with me a book written by Drunvalo called *Living in the Heart*, in which he repeatedly refers to physical darkness as a means of awakening the inner vision and the sacred place within the heart. I was fascinated. This darkness was just what I had been experiencing during my kayakalpa retreat!

Drunvalo also speaks about a torroidal forcefield surrounding the heart, which was an extension of the Merkaba. Is this the same forcefield I had been shown during my kayakalpa retreat? He draws this forcefield as two doughnut-shaped torroidal spheres nestled one inside the other. Does this forcefield explain why I had been guided to do the Holographic Merkaba breath twice at each stage of expansion, once for each of these torroidal spheres?

The power of this Holographic Merkaba was so profound that we ended up incorporating this concept into all of our Ilahinoor sessions. After grounding the tube of light, the giver would finish the session by creating this Merkaba field twice around the receiver — once to activate the Merkaba rotating left, and again to activate the Merkaba rotating right. The Merkaba would then stabilize itself in its optimum rotational harmony. We also have been experimenting with incorporating this concept into self-healing, long-distance healing, and group healings.

To summarize: Place your hands on your own heart, make a link to the heart chakra of the receiver, take a deep breath, and expel it forcefully while moving your hands rapidly in a circle out and around the receiver's body. Do this twice. This movement activates a forcefield around the receiver and opens a doorway to multidimensional consciousness.

It is not necessary to visualize anything. The heart is connected to the wisdom of the body, which knows exactly what to do without interference from the thinking mind. Remain in the experience of this field as long as you wish.

chapter 19

Diagonal Treatments

As we enter deeper into the vibrations of the Golden Age, we are beginning to shift away from self-imposed limitations toward divine mastery. No rules or limits dictate how far we can go. If any of you feel called to experiment with Ilahinoor as a system for healing and awakening, or to combine it with a healing system you already use, please do so.

There is a difference between *Ilahinoor* as a morphogenetic field of light and the *Ilahinoor treatment*, which refers to specific techniques for accessing this field. As long as we connect with the Ilahinoor field, what techniques we use do not really matter. The Basic Treatment and the Holographic Merkaba are good tools for anchoring this field into the body. Later, we found other ways to bring this energy in deeper. I will offer a few of these techniques as we go along, but please don't get attached to specific forms. These are guidelines rather than rules; they are continually evolving. In each case, please look to your higher self for more specific guidance.

In the *ayurvedic* tradition, three kinds of energy flows can be utilized in hands-on healing — vertical, horizontal, and diagonal. The diagonal flows, which stimulate the flow of Kundalini moving up the spine, are the most powerful. In order to deepen the integration of this cosmic energy, we first began to work with the thirteen major joints in a diagonal sequence, ending by grounding both feet together.

We would start with the Basic Treatment up until the heart activation, go through the diagonal sequence, and then continue with the rest of the Basic Treatment, ending with the Holo-graphic Merkaba.

One on one - Joint treatment

Start with the Basic Treatment – soul merge, Ilahinoor bridge, heart activation. Then, with the receiver lying down on a mas-sage table or the floor, use your hands to make the following connections.

1. Back of neck and left elbow
2. Left elbow and right wrist
3. Back of neck and right elbow
4. Right elbow and left wrist
5. Both wrists together to balance left and right sides
6. Right shoulder and left hip
7. Left hip and right knee
8. Right knee and left ankle
9. Left ankle and right wrist
10. Left shoulder and right hip
11. Right hip and left knee
12. Left knee and right ankle
13. Right ankle and left wrist
14. Both ankles together to ground the energy

Complete with pinkie, tube of light, and Holographic Merkaba

In the course of sharing this diagonal treatment in one of our workshops, I met Alberto and Giulia, two healers from Sardinia, Italy. This treatment reminded them of a sequence they had learned from the well-known Cypriot healer, Daskalos, which included the joints as well as the jaw, lymph nodes under the arms, liver, and spleen. We incorporated this sequence into the work with amazing results. The lymph nodes, liver, and spleen are useful for detoxification of the body, and seemed to great-ly support the rest of the diagonal work.

As with the previous treatment, each set of points is held on the opposite side of the body in order to stimulate the Kundalini flow along the spine. The giver and receiver sit on chairs facing each other. As the giver moves from one position to another, the receiver is receptive to whatever energies she or he is experiencing. For the sake of brevity, I am assuming that the sequence is clear enough not to explicitly mention receiver or giver in each step.

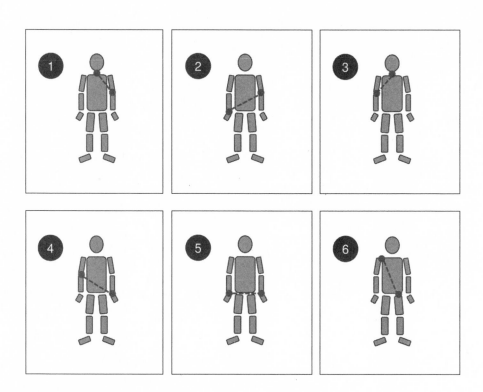

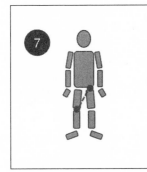
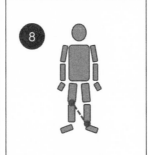
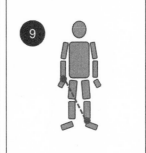
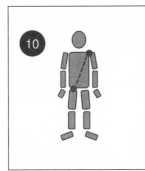
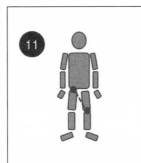
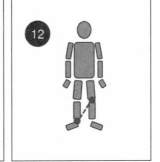
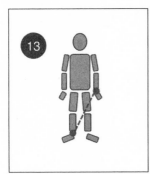
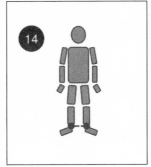

One on one – Extended diagonal treatment

Begin with soul merge, Ilahinoor bridge, and heart activation. Then move on to the diagonal sequence with your hands connecting with the receiver as follows:

1. Back of neck with right jaw
2. Right jaw with left shoulder
3. Left shoulder with lymph nodes under right arm
4. Right underarm with spleen area
5. Spleen with right hip
6. Right hip with back of left knee
7. Left knee with right ankle
8. Right ankle with left wrist
9. Both wrists together
10. Back of neck with left jaw
11. Left jaw with right shoulder
12. Right shoulder with lymph node under left arm
13. Left underarm with liver area
14. Liver with left hip
15. Left hip with back of right knee
16. Right knee with left ankle
17. Left ankle with right wrist
18. Both ankles together

The giver then places his/her hands on the soles of receiver's feet, channeling Earth energy up into receiver's body. This uploading of Earth energy is an important counterpart with which to end the treatment, since we have so far been working with downloading cosmic energy. Follow this up with the pinkie activation, tube of light, and Holographic Merkaba.

Hold each set of points until you feel a flow or pulsing of light. When it is time to make the diagonal between knee and ankle, it may be useful for the giver to pick up the receiver's leg and place it over his/her own leg, maintaining this position for the ankle-wrist diagonal as well. This position keeps the back straight and is more comfortable.

The link between the ankle and the wrist on both sides is especially important because this link connects all the meridians of the body, six of which move through the ankle and six of which move through the wrist.

One benefit of this treatment is that it also stimulates each of the chakras in turn. The Ilahinoor bridge stimulates the crown and third eye, the jaw-shoulder hold stimulates the throat chakra, the shoulder-underarm hold stimulates the heart chakra, the underarm with spleen/liver stimulates the solar plexus, the spleen/liver with hip stimulates the sacral chakra, and the hip-knee hold stimulates the root chakra.

This treatment can also be done on a massage table with the receiver lying down and the giver sitting alongside on a chair. It can also be done with two givers, mirroring each other on the diagonals!

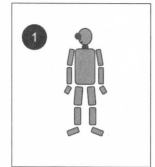
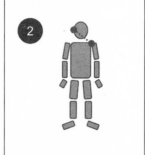
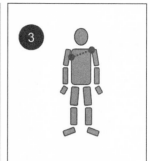

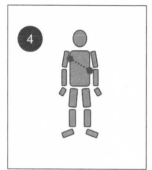
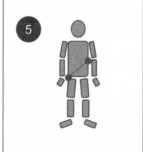
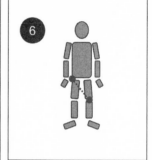

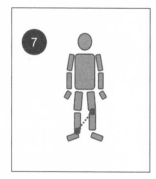
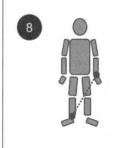
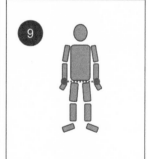

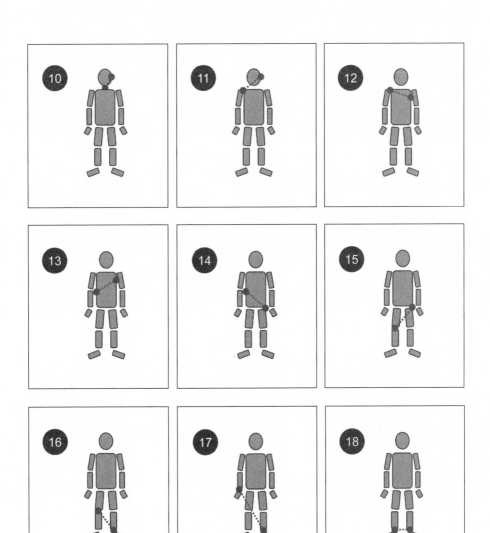

Instructions for a self-treatment are as follows:

Diagonal Self-Treatment

1. Connect with your higher self and guides as you attune to the morphogenetic field of Divine Light. Feel this light descending through the crown as a gentle golden rain.

2. Make the Ilahinoor bridge on yourself, touching the Ilahinoor points on the back of the head with one hand while placing your other hand on the forehead and crown area. After the first few times, placing your entire hand on the back of the head may be easier. Once you are familiar with the energy, you may find that you do not need the hand positions anymore.

3. Continue with the heart activation.

4. Start the diagonal sequence, hold the diagonal positions on yourself in whatever sequence feels comfortable, incorporating the back of the neck, jaw, shoulder, underarm, liver/spleen, hips, knees, ankles, wrists, and elbows. Include both sides of the body.

5. End with tube of light and Merkaba activation.

6. Lie down comfortably, perhaps with relaxing music, and give yourself time to integrate this energy. Breathe deeply and rhythmically.

7. A good time to practice Ilahinoor on yourself is immediately upon awakening, while you are still halfway in the dream worlds of the subconscious mind. You may find that the experience is stronger if you maintain the same body position as when you first wake up. You can also use Ilahinoor to program your dream state while falling asleep. Experiment with the diagonal positions while continuing to lie in bed!

chapter 20

Spinal Treatment

A healthy spine creates a healthy body. Besides the spine itself, there are spinal nerves branching out from each vertebra, which themselves connect with every single part of the body. The cerebro-spinal fluid moves through the spinal column between the cranium and the sacrum, keeping the nervous system in balance. There are also Kundalini channels situated along the spine that govern the life force moving through our bodies and link us to our higher bodies, through the chakra system.

With all the physical and emotional stresses of our daily lives, the spine often takes the impact. Doing some Ilahinoor work with the spine can therefore be a deeply soothing and energizing experience.

One way to work is simply to start with the Basic Treatment, and then work with each vertebra, gently applying pressure first on one side, then on the other side, and then slightly inward. It is important to be very sensitive here, as strong pressure on the spinal column can often be painful and damaging.

An easier and perhaps more effective treatment was shown to me by my friend Sophia Hildebrand from Stuttgart, Germany. We start with the soul merge, Ilahinoor bridge, and heart activation, as with most Ilahinoor treatments. Then, we find a point in the side of the neck directly below the bottom of each earlobe. These are access points into the spinal column.

There are numerical codes connected with each of the vertebrae. For example, the code for the atlas, which is the first cervical vertebra, is *121-10* or *one two one dash one zero*. The code for the axis, which is the second cervical vertebra, is *121-20* pronounced as *one two one dash two zero*. There are thirty-three vertebrae along the spine, which can be adjusted energetically through these earlobe points by mentally visualizing these codes while focusing on the different vertebrae.

The spinal cord consists of thirty-three vertebrae, which are usually categorized as follows:

7   cervical vertebrae, C1-C7

12   thoracic vertebrae, T1-T12

5   lumbar vertebrae, L1-L5

5   sacral vertebrae, which are fused together to form the sacrum

4   coccygeal vertebrae, which are fused together to form the coccyx or tailbone

The codes for each of these vertebrae go consecutively from top to bottom, starting with *121-10* (*one two one dash one zero*), going up ten for each successive vertebra, and ending with *121-330* (*one two one dash thirty-three zero*). Thus, for example, C3 corresponds with 121-30, T5 corresponds with 121-120, and L1 would be 121-200. The tip of the tailbone would be 121-330.

If you have specific problems with any of these vertebrae, simply hold the earlobe points while visualizing the corresponding code, and let the Ilahinoor energy do the work; or, simply go down the entire spine by numerical codes, either on yourself or on another person, continuing to hold the earlobe points.

Another way to work with the spine is to apply a gentle vibrating movement over the spine. If you were working with a partner, stand on one side of the receiver, who is seated on a stool. Starting with the neck, place your palms next to each other sideways over the top of his or her spine, thumbs touching each other. The padded area of the palm just below your fingers is making firm contact with the spinal column.

Gently vibrate your hands, letting the movement emanate from your entire body. It's a gentle vibration, not so much a shaking as a trembling. Continue this movement for a minute or two, then stop and let the energy integrate in stillness for another minute or two. Move on down to the next position along the spine and do the same thing. Continue down again to the bottom part of the spine and do the same thing. For most people, three hand positions will cover the entire spine, although if your hands are small or the person is exceptionally tall, it may take a fourth hand position.

End with lightly holding the middle finger of one hand on the tailbone, and the middle finger of your other hand on the crown. Stay with this position until you feel an energy pulsation, which means the cerebro-spinal fluid is flowing smoothly between the cranium and the sacrum.

You may combine the codes with the vibration, as in the following treatment:

Spinal Treatment

1. Receiver sits on stool, with giver sitting or standing to one side

2. Start with soul merge, Ilahinoor bridge, and heart activation

3. Holding the earlobe points with the middle fingers of each hand, visualize the codes for the first three vertebrae one by one, *121-10* for the atlas, *121-10* for the axis, and *121-30* for the third cervical vertebra.

4. Then, placing the palms of both hands sideways on the receiver's neck area, thumbs touching each other, gently start the vibration. Continue for one or two minutes

5. Hold still for a minute or two

6. Move down the spine to the next spine position and start the vibration. Continue for one or two minutes

7. Hold still for a minute or two

8. Move down to the next spine position and start the vibration. Continue for one or two minutes

9. Hold still for a minute or two

10. Place the middle finger of one hand lightly on the crown chakra, with the other hand connecting lightly to the tailbone of the receiver. This position activates the cerebro-spinal fluid, and grounds the energy through the central channel into the Earth

11. Finish with pinkie activation, tube of light, and Holographic Merkaba

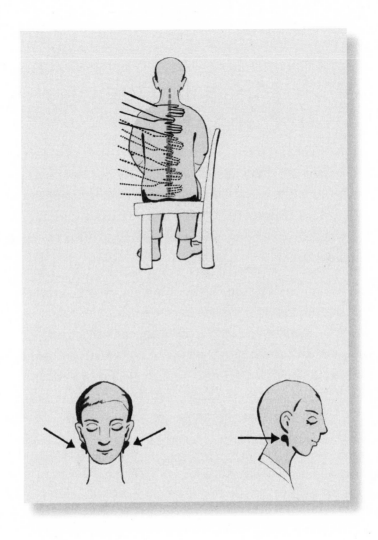

chapter 21

Miscellaneous Treatments

As we shared the Ilahinoor work in various settings, we continued to experiment with various treatment patterns, many of which were created by participants who were simply following their intuitive guidance, or had experience in other forms of healing practices.

We experimented with circle healings, where several people would work together on one person lying in the center of the circle. We experimented with long-distance healings and initiations. We practiced combining Ilahinoor with other healing modalities such as Reiki, Deeksha, Reconnection, Polarity Therapy, Quantum Touch, Pranic Healing, Bodytalk, EFT, Matrix Energetics, and Russian Healing. We worked with people who were experiencing various kinds of physical or psychological addictions. We worked with people who were birthing or dying.

Although it helps in the beginning to work with a partner or in a group, all of these treatments can also be done individually. We experimented with people calling in the energy on their own, sitting or lying in meditation, breathing gently and fully, holding the points on their own heads if they felt the need to, letting the energy pour through as a liquid golden light directly from their Higher Self. They could hold a specific intention if they wished, or simply surrender to their higher self to guide the process.

I would like to emphasize again that the Ilahinoor initiations come directly from the morphogenetic fields of light, and not from any human source. One candle can light many candles, and each of these candles can light many more. Ilahinoor is a gift from the gods, and I would not like to see any hierarchical organizations being created around this cosmic energy, nor for it to be misused for excessive financial gain.

Below is a sample of other possible treatments:

One on One – Simultaneous Treatment

In this treatment, the two partners work on each other simultaneously. Sitting close together, both lean forward until their foreheads touch at the third eye, while each places one finger of each hand on the Ilahinoor points of the other person. This position can create a very powerful connection between the two partners, and is especially beautiful when there is already closeness between the two. Interestingly, this position can also be very healing for a couple when they are in the middle of a verbal or emotional conflict.

One on One - Crown Adjustment

Place your hand in a blessing position over the receiver's head, either physically touching or held slightly away from the body. Invoke the Ilahinoor energy through your Higher Selves and feel a down-pouring of light entering at the crown chakra. Experiment with subtle movements to adjust this download as needed.

One on One – Foot Treatment

For someone whose Kundalini is already active, a good way of grounding and integrating the energy is for the giver to hold the bottom of the receiver's feet, inviting the cosmic light in through the crown of the receiver, and magnetically attracting it all the way down the body to the soles of his or her feet. Then reverse the flow, feeling energy from the Earth below pouring in through the soles of the feet, filling the body up to the head. Remain in this position for twenty to thirty minutes, or until the energy feels fully grounded and balanced. This treatment can also be very powerful for someone who is tired, stressed, or experiencing a Kundalini overload.

One on One – Off the Body Treatment

With practice, distinguishing various layers within the energy field of the receiver becomes easy. For example, the etheric double extends a few centimeters out from the physical body, while the emotional body extends out approximately one meter beyond the skin. The mental body may extend two or three meters out, and various layers of the soul body may extend out much further.

In this treatment, the practitioner remains standing above the receiver, who is lying comfortably at ground level. Work with these energy fields as intuitively guided, using the hands to connect with the subtle fields and harmonizing them. You may find yourself moving further and further away from the physical body as you harmonize subtler and subtler layers of the field.

It is recommended that you do the Basic Treatment a few times before attempting this more advanced treatment.

Proxy Treatment

If the intended receiver is not physically present, someone who is physically present can serve as a proxy for that person. Working on the proxy, the practitioner not only helps the proxy but also allows this divine light to be transmitted very effectively across a physical distance to the person for whom it is intended. This treatment can be especially helpful if a strong positive connection exists between the receiver and the proxy.

Group Treatment

This method is one of my favorite ways of working with Ilahinoor. One person lies down on a massage table or on a comfortable mat, with several others making a circle around the receiver holding diagonal positions over the joints. It helps to have one person cradling the head, and another grounding the feet. Include the chakras, if you wish, and any specific problem areas.

If it is too awkward to stretch diagonally across the receiver's body, and depending on the number of people in the circle, experiment with linking shoulder to hip, and wrist to knee, simultaneously on both sides of the body. For example, if eight people are in the circle, one person can lie down to receive, with one person at the head and another at the feet. One person may sit on the right side, connecting shoulder and hip, while another makes a connection between wrist and knee; this position will be mirrored by two people on the left side. The eighth person would simply connect the heart and solar plexus chakras.

The receiver states his or her intention for the healing, and the circle responds by channeling the Ilahinoor light to support this intention. After a few minutes, the givers slowly lift their hands away from the physical body, giving the receiver a couple of minutes to integrate. Group members then rotate positions around the circle in such a way that everybody gets a turn at each position.

Circle Healing

This method is a simple and playful way to share the Ilahinoor energy with a group of people. Everybody stands in a circle, and then makes a half turn so they are all facing the same direction. Place your hands on the person in front of you while receiving a blessing from the person behind you.

Gazing Circle

Here the intent is simply to sit within a circle of people and call in the Ilahinoor light with each participant holding eye contact with one other participant for as long as feels right. Either participant within a partnership may break eye contact whenever desired, go within to integrate the energy, and then move on to another participant in the circle. This is a powerful exercise for quickly entering into deep states of unified consciousness.

Group Soul Treatment

This is an amazingly powerful transmission of light that happens by simply attuning with the *group soul* of any group of people gathered together with focused intention. The same chakra system that is activated by the Ilahinoor field for an individual can be activated on the level of this group soul. When the crown, heart, and Earth chakras of a group are activated in this way, the energies can flow very profoundly through the entire group without the need for individual physical transmissions. This treatment is more advanced, and requires the practitioner to have developed a certain degree of unification within the subtle bodies, and to be able to withstand large amounts of divine light channeling through the body.

Higher Dimensional Transmissions

Once you have learned to work with the Ilahinoor field and your access to the higher self is established, giving an Ilahinoor session becomes even simpler. You simply make a clear request to your higher dimensional self and then let go, allowing the transmission to happen by itself. I first realized this would happen when I was asked to give a long distance Ilahinoor healing, promised to do so, and then forgot. To my surprise, the person called me the next day thanking me for what she described as a very profound experience!

When the same thing happened on a couple of other occasions, I realized that soul intention comes from a different place than mental intention. As our physical bodies become increasingly merged with our subtle bodies, our intentions become a gate through which higher dimensional energies can flow directly from the source field to whichever persons or situations our attention is directed toward. The more connected I AM with my inner being, the more this unified light can flow wherever it chooses to go, blessing each other and our planet in accordance with a higher evolutionary plan!

Saturday Morning Ilahinoor

Many of us around the world have been experimenting with energizing the Ilahinoor field on Saturday mornings at whatever time we are awake and ready to transmit. We invite people to join us if they wish, and also to receive an Ilahinoor initiation if they need to, whether for physical healing, emotional well-being, spiritual awakening, or for assistance in manifesting material needs in accordance with a divine plan. Focusing attention together in this way helps to strengthen the morphogenetic field of unified light for the entire planet.

Ilahinoor for Birthing and Dying

Ilahinoor helps to open the doorway between worlds. As such, it can be a beautiful experience for everyone involved to hold this space of unified light as a loved one makes the passage from one dimensional state to another, whether in birth or in death. It can also be useful to assist someone who is making a shamanic journey by holding him in this state of expanded unified awareness!

I was halfway across the world in Switzerland when my father died from heart failure. The night before his passage, I had been relaxing at a friend's home when I felt an enormous light enfolding my entire body, filling me with a deep sense of peace and ecstasy. I felt somehow that this feeling had to do with my father, even though I had no inkling of his impending heart attack. When my brother called me with the news the following morning, I was shocked and saddened, but not surprised. I had felt the night before that he was ready to go and that he was being guided smoothly and joyfully into the light.

chapter 22

Addiction and Trauma Release

Very few of us are truly free. If our nervous system were totally open and our subconscious mind completely clear, we would be capable of making free choices and living in full presence; however, most of us are crippled by traumas, concepts, phobias, and addictions that keep us trapped in a loop of conditioned feelings, thoughts, and behaviors.

Our subconscious mind is magnetically linked to a massive morphogenetic field that encompasses the entire history of humanity. We inherit certain tendencies simply by being born into human bodies — what Christians refer to as *original sin*. The stronger this morphogenetic field becomes, the more it controls our lives, and the less freedom we have. Our political, economic, and social systems, by whatever names we choose to label them, are a direct reflection of this loss of freedom.

Earlier in this book, I referred to the geomagnetic reversal and its potential to reboot the operating system of human consciousness. This event would be a time when the entire subconscious slate of human conditioning could be wiped out, giving us an opportunity to start over as a new species, connected directly to our multidimensional presence.

But perhaps we don't have to wait for this geomagnetic reversal in order to begin our journey back to freedom. The superconscious power of the Ilahinoor work is a potent antidote to *original sin*. It is a means of regaining our *original innocence* by demagnetizing the subtle conditioning of our subconscious mind. This work can be especially useful in the field of trauma and addiction release by combining it with some elements of *rapid eye movement* technology.

Researchers have noticed that when we dream, our eyes move back and forth rapidly beneath their closed lids. It is possible that nature uses these rapid eye movements to release stressful events of the day. The same principle can be applied to waking life.

Various therapies evolved in the United States in the 1970s to deal with post-traumatic stress in war veterans returning home from Vietnam. Among these were rapid eye movement therapies, which proved to be very effective. It was found that when we move our eyes rapidly from side to side, nerve signals cross the corpus collosum dividing the two hemispheres of the brain, which allows trauma patterns held in the nervous system to unravel. I would like to share a method that borrows some elements from these therapies, and combines them with the Ilahinoor work.

As you prepare to work with clients, first identify in a few words what they wish to release. It could be addiction to substances such as tobacco, narcotics, or alcohol. It could be addictive behaviors or relationships, attachments or aversions. It could be traumas related to birth, early childhood, accidents, or war. It could be emotional patterns and defense mechanisms. It could be various kinds of physical or emotional fears and phobias. Focus on something that is visibly affecting their life at this particular time.

Now have them feel this condition as fully as possible in the body. Have them imagine a scale from one to ten. How deeply is this condition affecting their lives at this time? What number comes to mind?

Now start the Ilahinoor treatment with them. Go through the soul merge, Ilahinoor bridge, and heart activation. Next have them do a round of rapid eye movements. Sitting across from them, move your finger back and forth across their line of vision, and have them follow it with their eyes. You should be at a comfortable distance so they don't have to squint, and do not move so fast that they can't follow. It's like the movement of a windshield wiper on a car. Experiment with approximately one second per swipe.

After a couple minutes of rapid eye movement, have them close their eyes, feel what is going on in their bodies, then ask them again how they feel the intensity of this addiction or trauma on a scale of one to ten. They might experience some shaking or trembling, spontaneous deep breathing, or emotional release.

Go back to the Ilahinoor bridge and heart activation, following up with another round of eye movements. Continue this exercise several times, each time having them feel what's going on in their bodies and noticing the intensity of the trauma or addiction on a scale of one to ten. Continue until they are down to a manageable number on the scale. Often, you may notice that the number first goes higher before it comes down.

Complete the session with the pinkie activation, tube of light, and Holographic Merkaba to lock in the new frequencies. After this stage, have them dance, shake, or vibrate their entire bodies to release the nervous system.

If you yourself are dealing with a trauma or addiction you would like to release, it is best to practice this technique with someone you trust who can hold space for you to go through whatever you need to go through. Sometimes two or more sessions may be needed, spaced a few days apart. If you feel comfortable doing it with yourself, for example if you wish to quit smoking, you can simply do self-Ilahinoor sessions by shifting your eyes back and forth between two objects spaced on either side of your line of vision.

A little story I'd like to share may be relevant here. There are five chapters to this story. In chapter one, you are walking down a road. There is a big hole in the middle of the road. You don't see it, and you fall in. You refuse to take personal responsibility for the act, blaming everyone, and everything you can possibly think of. It takes you forever to climb out!

In chapter two, you are walking down the same road. There is a big hole in the middle of the road. You fall in, but this time you realize it was your fault. Your anger toward the rest of the world gets turned inward. You stop blaming others but start judging yourself. It's still not easy, but eventually you climb out.

In chapter three, you are walking down the same road. There is a big hole in the middle of the road. You see it, but by now it has become a habit, so of course you fall in. You take responsibility without blame or judgment, and just as quickly, you climb back out.

In chapter four, you are walking down the same road. There is a big hole in the middle of the road. But you walk around it.

In chapter five, you walk down a different road!

Our journey in life is about moving from chapter one to chapter five. As we clear out subconscious patterns, traumas, and addictions, we notice that we have more choices. Rather than being trapped in the past or in the future, we can live in a state of deeper presence. We don't need to be victims of our — or anyone else's — drama.

As we proceed along this journey of awareness, we find that we don't require the same traumas and challenges anymore. We can grow with beauty, ease, fluidity, and grace. Things come easily, and we find ourselves increasingly in the right place at the right time. We can live our lives from a space of joyful freedom and service. We learn to walk down a different road!

chapter 23

Planetary Linking

The Holographic Merkaba is a means of linking our divine intent to the collective field of human and Earth evolution. The following chapter describes a meditation that can be used individually or in groups to help facilitate this experience.

This meditation was first devised for use with groups after my first experience of swimming with whales, and later modified after experiencing the Holographic Merkaba. It is a powerful practice for linking spherically to aspects of ourselves that are beyond human form and consciousness. As we holographically connect with these aspects of ourselves, we enter into powerful states of creator-consciousness, able to effectively seed new possibilities for ourselves and for our planet.

We are simultaneously galactic beings and human beings. As we sit here now with part of our consciousness actively inhabiting these physical bodies, another part of our consciousness is simultaneously soaring through infinite galaxies in creative play. In this meditation, we will go through a process of holographic linking, first connecting with the soul of the Earth and with all the kingdoms of the Earth. Then, we will travel out, connecting with the Sun and galaxies beyond, merging into galactic and cosmic consciousness.

This practice is powerful for planetary healing work. If you are facilitating this practice for a group, you may wish to make a recording of this meditation, at least when doing it for the first time, perhaps accompanied by soothing whale music. Once you are familiar with the basic technique, please modify it as you feel guided from within.

---○---

As you breathe, let your breath become circular, breathing in and breathing out in a slow, regular rhythm. Become aware of your body, of sensations within your body. Notice where you experience the center of gravity within your body. Become aware of sensations: tingling or pulsing, tightness or pain, expansion or contraction, heat or cold. Wherever energy is directed, it creates a corresponding change in cellular awareness. Each cell requires only attention, a focus of energy, in order to resonate to its highest potential. So bring your awareness, part by part, throughout your body, aware of whatever sensations come up.

Now, become aware of your body as a whole. Become aware of your posture. And then, as if you were a tree, feel your roots going into the Earth, going through the floor, through the foundation of the building, through the topsoil, and through the various layers of soil and rock. Move through underground streams of water, hollow spaces, and magma. Let yourself go deeper and deeper, layer by layer, with each breath getting closer to the heart of the Earth Mother. It is as if you were following a golden cord connecting you to the very core of the Earth so that you can receive her life force directly from her heart.

Feel the heart of the Earth Mother. With each cycle of breath, open to this pulse coming up from the Earth. As you inhale, receive these pulses into every cell in the body. As you exhale, release any tightness, contraction, fear or pain, sending it down the tube of light, back down that root system into the center of the Earth to be transmuted in her cosmic fire. The heart of the Earth is a cosmic fire. It is a flame that connects to the flame within the Sun. Inner doorways connect from Earth's inner Sun to our solar Sun, then through our Sun to the Galactic Sun, and through the Galactic Sun to the Universal Sun of Creator-Consciousness. The entire universe is interdimensionally linked.

Within the fire of the Sun are the geometric codes for our soul's growth and evolution. Through the heart of the Earth below as well as the heart of the Sun above, these codes can be received into each cell of our bodies, which is also a Sun. In the nucleus of each cell is that same radiant energy that lies within the nucleus of the Earth, or the nucleus of the Sun, or the nucleus of a Galaxy.

And so, with your breath, receive now this luminous quality of light, the healing gift of the Earth. Breathe it up into your bodies, up into the heart and then up through the tube of light into the Sun overhead. In from below, up to the heart, out to the Sun above.

Then reverse this flow, breathing in from the Sun down the tube of light, feeling a stream of liquid light entering through the crown and flooding every cell with frequencies of light. Breathe this light into your heart, and then down to the center of the Earth. Continue going back and forth from Earth to Sun, Sun to Earth for a few breaths, allowing your breath to become very slow and subtle.

It is as if you were a tree with your roots going deep into the Earth, and your branches reaching up to the Sun. Each leaf, each branch is an antenna for prana, or life force energy. So, as you feel the exchange of energy up and down the tube of light, become aware also that you are receiving prana directly through your skin. Every pore of your skin is alive to prana. You are breathing in prana through your skin. You are breathing in prana from the Soul star above your head, and from the Earth star below your feet.

And now, with your next breath, you are going to breathe all the way in from both directions, simultaneously filling your heart with the pranic energies of both Sun and Earth. You will then be extending the Holographic Merkaba seeded within your own heart out into your aura.

As you breathe in, bring your hands up in prayer position to the heart. Then, as you breathe out, expel your breath forcefully, simultaneously moving your hands out in a rapid motion to trace your aura out and around the body, then back to the heart.

So breathe in fully now, and then OUT, forcefully expelling your breath like the spouting of a whale. Feel the Holographic Merkaba locking into place around you. Wait a few breaths, then prepare for another activating breath. Breathe in fully, and then OUT, once again expelling your breath with a popping sound and feeling the energy build around you.

Feel the energy of this Holographic Merkaba. Over the next few breaths, feel how your aura begins to radiate out to merge with the group soul. As you experience this merging, the chakra system of the group soul becomes a tube of light with its diameter being the entire circle. As you connect with the group soul, notice what you experience in the Ilahinoor points in the back of the head. Notice if you feel a throbbing or pulsing. Stay there for a minute or two, and notice if you feel a deepening with your identity as a group soul.

Invoke any higher-dimensional masters, avatars, guides, or angels that you wish, and notice as the room becomes thick with presence. Become aware of a sound current, a frequency of sound that begins to permeate the head and, eventually, the whole body. It could be a low humming. It could be a high-frequency pitch. It could be the buzzing of bees, or the sound of a conch, or of rushing waters. It could be very subtle, or so loud that it drowns out everything else. It could change from time to time. Listen. Listen deeply. This is the sound of your soul as it anchors into physical form, into your physical circuitries.

Notice that as you link in as a group soul, the sound current becomes louder and stronger. There is a deeper stillness because the energy bodies go further out. Now, as you prepare for the next round of breath, you will be working with the tube of light of this group soul, as wide around as the diameter of this circle.

So breathe in now from the heart of the Earth Mother, up through this expanded pillar of light into the heart chakra of this group soul, and then up the pillar of light to the Sun. And then, breathe in from the Sun down to the group heart, continuing down into the Earth. Continue breathing until you feel a solid anchoring below and above, from Earth below to Sun above.

Now breathe in simultaneously from above and from below into the group heart, bringing your hands into position, getting ready to project them out with the next exhale. Expel your breath forcefully now as you breathe OUT, activating the Holographic Merkaba of the group soul... Once again now, breathing in, then OUT.

As your energy bodies continue to expand over the next few breaths, feel yourself merging with the larger community or bioregion. Feel your sense of identity merging with other resonant humans in this community, known and unknown. Feel yourself merging with the spirits of nature — with the devas, the fairies, the mountain spirits, the elves, the water sprites, the plant people, the animal people, the bird tribes. Listen for the whale songs connected to this particular area of the planet. Listen to the sound current again, letting yourself blend with this larger group soul.

Continuing to let your breath be a circle, you are now breathing up and down this enormous passage of light that may be tens of miles in diameter. Notice how much easier it gets to anchor the frequency codes from the Sun and from the Galactic Center. We serve as an anchor for these frequency codes, cosmic energies from around the universe, anchoring them all the way down into the subtle bodies of Earth, using our own bodies as a bridge.

And now, with your next breath you will breathe in simultaneously from the Sun above and the Sun below into the heart of this city or bioregion. As you breathe out, you will activate the Holographic Merkaba of this region. Breathe in now, and OUT.

Feel yourself merging for hundreds of miles in every direction now, merging with the trees in the forests, with the lakes, rivers, and streams, with mountain ranges, plateaus, and valleys. You are merging consciousness with all the beings of this bioregion: human, animal, devic, angelic, all those in alignment with these visions of peace and beauty, creativity and joy, love and healing. Let these visions, these qualities, be felt through this entire collective now as you feel your collective soul merging with the entire country, wherever you are.

Feel the whales again blending into your consciousness. Blend into their consciousness and weave through their song lines with your own visions of new possibilities. As you continue breathing in, connect with the heart of the Earth through a massive river of light, the size of this entire country. Bring up the sacred Earth energies into the collective consciousness of this nation, and then send it out to the Sun. Send out our intentions from our Sun out to the Galactic Sun, and then even farther out to the central codes of creation within the Universal Sun.

There is a response that flows back to us now. It flows down this great river of light from the Universal Sun, stepping down through all the Suns, and into the heart of this nation, and anchoring within the Earth. Again, bring your awareness into the sound current to amplify the sense of union with the soul of this nation, letting your individualized boundaries dissolve.

Continue going up and down this great river of light. And now you are ready to expand once again, and this time you will connect with the soul of Gaia. Breathe in simultaneously from both directions into the unified heart of this nation and, breathing out, let your Holographic Merkaba expand to connect with the soul of Gaia; breathing in, and expelling OUT.

Feel your boundaries dissolving once again, as you let yourself become the body of the Earth, the soul of the Earth, the consciousness of the Earth. Let this feeling become your primary identity now. All beings in the entire web of life are within your body as Gaia now. Deepen this identity by focusing on the sound current, letting yourself move out into concentric circles, allowing the tube of light of the planet to be the north-south polar axis.

As you merge with the body of the Earth, breathe in through the South Pole. Feel yourself connect with the Source of All Creation. Breathe into the heart of the Earth Soul, and then as you breathe out, connect up through the North Pole to the center of our Milky Way galaxy. As you breathe in from the Galactic Center, receive the evolutionary energies of the galactic superwave coming our way, anchoring them into the subtle bodies of the Earth.

Hear the whales now spread out within the oceans of the Earth, each with their own unified song, creating and maintaining the light grids of Mother Earth. The whales are seeding these light grids with our collective thoughts and intentions for beauty, for peace, for joy, for awakening, for coming fully alive as a sacred planet, an ascended planet. Visualize this situation as already existing. Radiant, concentric spheres of light ripple out from the center of the planetary heart, permeating all fields, all dimensions, and all life within the body and soul of Gaia.

A new Earth is being created. A new species of humanity is being birthed. We are stepping into a higher dimensional world now, the Sixth Sun of the Mayas, a new Age of Light.

Within this morphogenetic field of light, we see a beautiful new world being born, beyond greed and destruction, beyond separation and war. The whales hold a memory of this world in times past and in a time to come. With them, and all the nature spirits, angelic orders, and galactic beings who are here with us, we plant this seed of memory into the light grids of our planet. We each have our role to play, and together we affirm that the Earth is once again sacred and whole.

As a group, you may wish to state your vision for this new creation with prayers that come from your heart, or simply by naming qualities such as "love," "awakening," and "beauty" out into the circle...

It is time now for our Holographic Merkaba to expand even further. Prepare to breathe in now from both directions along the polar axis into the heart of this planetary web of life. Breathe in, then expel OUT. Again: in, and OUT.

Feel yourselves merging now with the entire cosmos, expanding into the universe at warp speed, the stars and galaxies each but one cell within your cosmic body. There is endless space, limitless potential here. Your individual self, even your planetary self, has merged with your cosmic self.

Listen for the sound current now, which is your own note that you add to this great song of creation. Remain in this deep creative stillness for as long as you wish.

———○———

This concludes my own writings on Ilahinoor. The rest of this book includes chapters from other Ilahinoor practitioners who have been experimenting with these energies over the years, each in their own unique way. My websites, Kiarawindrider.net, Ilahinoor.net, and Deekshafire.com, include additional compilations of people's experiences with this energy, as well as additional guidelines for practice. Please check for updates from time to time, and feel free to post your own experiences as well.

PART IV

FURTHER CONTRIBUTIONS TO ILAHINOOR

I am a point of light within a greater light
I am a strand of loving energy
within the stream of love divine
I am a spark of sacrificial fire focused
within the fiery will of God
And thus I stand
I am a way by which my brothers and sisters may achieve
I am a source of strength enabling them to stand
I am a beam of light shining upon their way
And thus I stand
And standing thus resolve
To tread this way the ways of the world
And know the ways of God
And thus I stand
And thus I stand
And thus I stand

— Tumi, The Disciple's Prayer (adapted from Alice Bailey)

chapter 24

Call of the Sky Mother

by Grace Sears

Grace and I have shared many beautiful journeys over the years. A mystic, mother, and cosmic explorer, she is committed to sharing with others the endless possibilities of our divine awakening. She currently lives in Turkey, and can be reached at gracesears1@ yahoo.com.

————○————

This current phase of my life started with what has come to be known as the *Deeksha movement*. From 2004 onwards, Kiara and I had worked practically nonstop bringing what we felt was our soul's calling, *Deeksha*, to people in Europe, India, and, for me, also in California and Hawaii. We were very much pioneers in the movement, and had started the work with a feeling of great excitement, sensing that this practice was a key to the collective awakening of humanity.

After a couple of years, we were discovering that often the powerful energies of Deeksha were remaining in the head centers and not being integrated into the rest of the body, causing some people an electrical over-stimulation of the brain, and an imbalance in the body's energy system. Others would experience a few moments or hours of peace, but then *ananda* would pass, leaving them feeling much the same as before. Contrary to our expectations, few people were experiencing permanent changes in awareness. The juice was there, but it seemed that most bodies could not fully assimilate it.

My own initiation with Deeksha in India had been so immensely powerful that I was unable to open my eyes for the intensity of the light. As if struck by lightning, I experienced burned spots on top of my head, nausea, and complete immobility. My central nervous system surged and burned for seven days, culminating with the Kundalini energy rising straight up through the crown. During the following eight months, I progressed from a newborn baby with a wide limitless perspective but minimal motor skills, to a functioning adult immersed in child-like innocence and joy.

I had felt sure that the power of the Deeksha was strong enough that everyone could feel this same depth of transformation and joy, and so we were absolutely dedicated to sharing this potential with as many people as possible; however, as the years went by, we found that the results were inconsistent, and that those unable to integrate these energies sometimes had emotional or physical imbalances.

For myself, with all the traveling and operating in a constant field of high frequency light, I was burning out physically.

I had been working for some months in Hawaii with Dean Nelson, who is a network chiropractor, doctor of Chinese medicine, and teacher of Tibetan Buddhism. We had many talks about how to allow the body greater access to the Deeksha light and to assimilate it in a way that we could sustain the benefits.

We gave some retreats together and had wonderful and lasting success combining our two modalities. I would give the Deeksha and then Dean would treat the spine with network chiropractic work. We worked also with movement, dance, and various forms of meditation. We found that the central nervous system responded beautifully, in a balanced and centered way, integrating the Deeksha energies throughout the human organism. Rather than a pleasant but temporary interlude of bliss, people were reporting lasting changes to their consciousness, relationships, and health.

During this same time, Kiara was in Dalyan, Turkey, where he had been doing an intensive retreat with four wonderful women, each holding a deep level of consciousness and commitment. All of them had experienced past life connections with ancient Egypt. Their combined presence became a chalice for a strong and powerful energy, which entered the room and identified itself as an ancient Egyptian deity named Ra. They were introduced to an ancient and universal morphogenetic field capable of initiating an alchemical transformation of dense physical matter so it could be permeated with light. This field came to be known as *Ilahinoor*, the Turkish name for *Divine Light*.

When I returned to Turkey, Kiara shared this new energy with me. I experienced it as Kundalini activating; it came from below, and moved upward, gentle and undulating, very centering and balancing. I saw it as a beautiful and efficient answer from the divine to balance the electrical stimulation of the Deeksha. The energy was more magnetic in nature, with a slower wave function than the quick high frequency of Deeksha, gliding through my physical body like butter. It was much simpler and more portable and immediate than carrying a doctor and chiropractic table with you!

Some months later, we were in Italy, teaching Ilahinoor to a group of one-hundred spiritual healers in Padova, many of whom had been working with Deeksha, and were asking us about the differences between them. In the powerful energy field created by this great group of healers, I could physically see Deeksha and Ilahinoor as two distinct streams of light, complementary and interweaving, and of course emanating from the same single Source. I felt that Ilahinoor had come as an answer to a need created by the powerful presence of the Deeksha energy, rather like the feminine aspect coming in to refine and harmonize the intensity of the masculine. It was not just a complement, but also an essential creative power in its own right, providing what the masculine cannot on its own.

It is interesting to see that the way Ilahinoor is introduced and transferred is also more feminine, without hierarchy or formal organization. No one takes the role of priest or shaman, guru or intermediary. One human being is simply lovingly present with another without agenda, and the energy envelops both. I feel this is an important aspect, *without agenda* — the mind is clear and empty of intention or desire or the need to accomplish anything. No money need change hands, and no one is more powerful or more able than the other. The *Course in Miracles* says, "All separation vanishes as holiness is shared. For holiness is power, and by sharing it, it gains in strength." Sharing Ilahinoor envelops us in holiness, allowing souls to meet, sweet and simple and true.

Recently, we were in Lelystad, Holland with a group of transcendental meditators, Deeksha givers, and Ilahinoor practitioners. During the first evening, we had planned to share a transmission of energy where anyone in the group could participate in giving as well as receiving. Since many in the group were Deeksha givers, the organizer suggested we could give either Deeksha or Ilahinoor as we felt. My suggestion was that we allow the light of the divine to flow through us without giving it a name or form, or in any way restricting or directing it with the mind, and to experience what that might be like, how it might be different from before.

I began in the old way, placing my hands on someone's head, but it felt restrictive — constraining to my body and to the energy. What felt right was to stand in front of the person with arms lowered and palms toward them, heart open, the entire aura and physical body emanating light and love and beauty, much like pictures we see of Mother Mary.

I experienced a rich and quiet bliss that I haven't known in quite this way. What I have learned is to be open to the moment, to what intuitively serves the person I am with, and the situation.

We have often said that the techniques around Ilahinoor are only the beginning; they are simply guidelines to help become familiar with the energy. Once we are familiar with the energy, we can simply allow it to express through us according to the need of the moment.

A huge expansion happened for me in Bolivia last autumn, when I had a profound experience on the Island of the Moon in Lake Titicaca. She is the feminine counterpart to the Island of the Sun, where it is believed that the Incas descended from the Sun god Inti. This island is where maidens would come to worship and to purify themselves. No one lives here; it is very high in altitude, about 12,700 ft, and crystal clear — with no thought forms or electromagnetic pollution.

Our Peruvian shaman, Tutto, was performing a powerful ceremony at an ancient ceremonial site on the crest of the island. During the ceremony, I was spoken to by a being, a field of being, who made herself known to me as Sky Mother. I was aware that she was known to Native American people; in fact they were waiting for the fulfillment of a prophecy in which she would return to them. She told me that I had come from her to help mend the tear in the fabric of the universe and to empower the Earth mothers to care for their own. I was shown a mesa in New Mexico where a Native American woman elder was standing waiting, heavily holding the burden of her people.

I did not know of Sky Mother or exactly what she meant by mending the tear in the fabric of the universe, or even by her last message that I must come back soon. But the energy field was so very high and clear and tremendously powerful that I had no doubt as to its validity — although I found myself constantly pondering the meaning of her message.

A week later, during another ceremony in the Amazon jungle of Peru, I was taken to Sky Mother — far, far out in the universe into a dark, full nothingness — pulsing with unimaginably immense compassion, the infinite potential of creation. As I watched, tiny particles coalesced to become a point of light within her. Detaching itself from her, the little point of light travelled unerringly through the universe, entering the pregnant belly of a woman on Earth. I humbly realized that I was seeing the arising of a human soul, birthed from the great Cosmic Mother.

I was taken from there to New Mexico, walking around the edge of the mesa toward the waiting Native American woman. I was sparkling, scintillating, light-filled, fresh from being with the Sky Mother, and walking toward the woman. As I stood in front of her, she burst into a ball of joyful, effervescent blue-gold light! The heaviness of her burden, and the fatigue of her physical being were transformed in a holy instant.

I took this joy, this light of empowerment of the Great Sky Mother to Chief Arvol Looking Horse, whom I had known in California some years ago. Chief Arvol is the carrier of the White Buffalo Calf Woman peace pipe, which we smoked together; and he is chief of the Sioux tribes. He has been working relentlessly to reunite his people and mend the sacred hoop; he carries a great sadness. I stood in front of him to share with him this joy, this light of the immensity of the Great Sky Mother; so that he would know her presence and be encouraged.

As I write this story, I feel again the magnitude, the richness of her formless being —awesome and unfathomable. There is nothing to say. There is nothing to do — only to show up empty and willing and let something greater emanate through that willingness — gracious willingness, as someone said to me years ago — or, perhaps the willingness to be Grace.

As the universe would have it, just as I sat to write this chapter, I discovered the work of Sharron Rose. She writes of the 2012 galactic alignment and the coming changes from a perspective that fills me with awe and delight!

She says that for the Egyptians, the center of the galaxy was symbolized by the great goddess Isis in her role as the mother of creation. She says that one of the great secrets of ancient Egypt is that the center of the galaxy is a secret Sun that exists behind our Sun. In alchemical language, it was called the black Sun, or the invisible Sun — *the secret Sun of the eternal feminine.*

Many spiritual traditions, including the Maya and Inca, speak of the great central Sun, or the Sun behind our Sun, a *stargate* through which our ancestors came to this galaxy, this solar system, this Earth.

Sharron talks also of Paul LaViolette and his theory of *galactic superwaves*, and of the cosmic rays pulsing now from the center of the galaxy. I feel that the new light technologies of recent years (Deeksha, Ilahinoor, Reconnection, etc.) are the effects of these cosmic rays and electromagnetic pulses as they move through the Earth planes. We are continuing to learn how to work with them for the evolution of humanity.

Sharrron says that everything that is — all of nature, human beings, and human consciousness — originally comes from this womb of the galaxy. If she is Isis, then our galactic center is the Great Mother, the creative feminine force from which everything emerges — her pregnant womb continuously giving birth to millions of stars. For the Egyptians, Isis is the creator of all things, a divine feminine force that bursts outward from the supreme source in glittering waves of luminosity that merge and shape themselves into material reality.

This perspective is beautiful for me, after my experience with Sky Mother in the heart of creation. How lovely to feel that after millennia of patriarchal control and abuse of nature, mother Earth, women, children, and feminine values everywhere, the coming change is the Mother Goddess returning, breathing her life and love and wonder back into this tired world. The powerful gamma waves and forces reported by our scientists are the evolutionary pulse, the heartbeat of our galaxy, of our Mother Goddess.

The Great Mother is also unmitigated power, not just as creator but as sustainer of life, and destroyer of obsolete forms and patterns. This power gives me hope and the certainty that we are, indeed, in good hands. Not only is she guiding our evolutionary journey, but she is also creating it. We will evolve into a more beautiful, compassionate species — or perish along the way.

The purpose of any path is to take us beyond itself, eventually returning us to where we began. We arrive at the beginning, seeing with new eyes, eyes filled with innocence born of wisdom, from a deep experience of life.

How we live in the day to day is what makes us a spiritual master, or a divine human — how filled with joy and playfulness, how appreciative of beauty and the wonder of nature. As we radiate kindness, acceptance, and contentment, we become a vessel of the Great Mother. We transform with our smile. We uplift with our presence. Thus, we fulfill our destiny. Thus, we take our place as creators and contributors to a new Earth filled with bounty, beauty, and love.

chapter 25

Our Journey
with Ilahinoor

by Barry Snyder and Karen Anderson

Karen Anderson and Barry Snyder have shared Ilahinoor through in-person groups and teleconferences for several years. The following account of their experiences with Ilahinoor is adapted from their book Agents of Grace. *For more about what Karen and Barry have experienced with Ilahinoor and how it has catalyzed the evolution of their awakening work, please visit their website, LuminousSelf.com.*

The Stage is Set

Kiara became a close friend during the time he lived in Mt. Shasta, CA. Over many years, we have shared countless discussions about this extraordinary time on the planet. Together, we've observed the breakdown of old hierarchical structures and paradigms, and breakthroughs into new ways of being. As fellow travelers in the great adventure of awakening, we have shared our discoveries and illuminations with one another along the way.

After twenty-two years in the U.S., Kiara returned to his motherland, India. A few months later, we received an excited email from him, relating that many people, including his partner, Grace, were experiencing profound awakenings after receiving something called *Deeksha*. This experience was taking place within the ashrams of someone called Kalki Bhagavan and his wife, Amma, who were said to be dual avatars of enlightenment. Knowing our lives are dedicated to awakening, Kiara finished his email with, "You might want to check this out."

A few months later, we traveled to Golden City for some of the first programs offered to Westerners by disciples of Amma/Bhagavan. There, we experienced a level of grace we had never before encountered. We witnessed a room full of 300 people catapulted into some of the most exalted awakenings we had ever experienced. The full account of receiving our first Deeksha can be found on our website; for now, suffice it to say that we left the ashram convinced the Deeksha offered a major upleveling in the process of birthing an awakened humanity. Although we had witnessed potent awakenings through the soul-awakening sessions we facilitated, here was a vehicle of grace through which large numbers of people could awaken — and quickly. The Deeksha, Bhagavan often said, was capable of catalyzing a collective awakening within the short period of time many felt our species had left before our many crises overwhelmed our abilities to transcend them.

The tremendous openings in consciousness that our first Deekshas delivered did not fade away; they became the ever-present backdrop of our awareness, resting just behind and beneath the continuously fluctuating states and conditions of everyday life. We had been propelled beyond the illusion of the separate self into a space of unity that was more palpably real than anything else in existence.

When we received our first Deekshas in 2004, only Bhagavan's disciples, or dasas, were empowered to give the transmission. But when Bhagavan announced that he would be releasing the capacity to pass on the Deeksha to people who were not dasas, we knew this work was our next step. We became Deeksha givers in 2005 and shared the Deeksha through ongoing, seven-month groups and other events.

Although we loved witnessing the powerful awakenings that many people experienced from the Deeksha, we didn't feel comfortable acting as intermediaries, dispensing grace that we had received through an intermediary. Acknowledging that throughout history gurus and teachers have led many to enlightenment, we also felt that the guru model tends to foster a subtle sense of separation that can actually thwart self-realization. We knew that, ultimately, all grace comes from the One Source, of which every one of us is an aspect. For us, self-realization means reawakening to our oneness with the Divine, merging with and fully embodying the One. This perspective led us to go directly to the Source and ask the Divine Light to pour through the Deeksha, rather than continuing to call to Amma/Bhagavan, as we had learned to do in India.

This change served to unhook not only us, but also recipients of the Deeksha, from the belief that intermediaries are necessary to receiving divine blessings. In addition, because everything we knew about how to facilitate awakening had been revealed directly, through sessions and inner experiences of the Divine, we had never followed anyone else's guidance or instruction. Now, we felt no inner prompting to become part of an organization, even one dedicated to oneness. We knew we were always to remain free agents for God, maintaining a sovereign, direct relationship to the Divine.

Because our work with people had proved that each of us is capable of directly connecting with the Divine, in our new role as Deeksha-givers we could not set ourselves up as exclusive sources of grace when we knew this role wasn't true. Our dream had always been to see all beings discover their capacity to directly receive divine grace. Initially, Bhagavan had promised that the ability to share the Deeksha would spontaneously arise in those who received it; but, although we encouraged this understanding in our groups, the idea never really caught fire. Nonetheless, we continued to hold fast to that dream, and prayed to take part in its fulfillment.

As always, the Source responds to a sincere, life-aligned request. We soon received emails from Kiara about a new energetic transmission that he and a group of friends had received during a retreat in Turkey. Intrigued by what he wrote, we arranged a time to talk by phone with our dear friend.

Our Introduction to Ilahinoor

During that phone conversation with Kiara in the Spring of 2007, Kiara described Ilahinoor as a soft, feminine energy that was very helpful in integrating the Deeksha. He happily described the easy, effortless way people spontaneously shared Ilahinoor with one another after receiving the transmission. The awakenings and transformations were of the same magnitude as the Deeksha, he indicated, which offered a major breakthrough in the potential for catalyzing planetary awakening.

Not only could people awaken quickly, but also they now didn't have to find an exclusive intermediary to access the source of grace. Even better, once they received and sufficiently integrated the frequencies of Ilahinoor, which might require a few transmissions, they, too, could pass it on. Each of us could participate in a potentially limitless sharing of the transmission.

This change was what we had been waiting for! With no limits on its use, Ilahinoor could go viral in no time, bringing its gifts to all who were interested in receiving them. The radical new possibility the Deeksha had introduced was going to its next level of unfoldment.

After we all hung up, Kiara transmitted Ilahinoor to us from his home in Turkey. Karen describes her initial experience:

I had a very powerful, palpable experience of the energies coming in through my face, and then descending into the body, primarily on the left side. They came with a great deal of swirling turbulence, like an unstable solution or the action of a washing machine. The energies swirled for some time in the face and head, then in the heart/throat/soul center area. They eventually moved down the left side into the second chakra area, where they stayed for a long time.

As the turbulence continued to churn, it left in its wake a feeling of absolute stillness in each area as it moved on. It finally came to rest in the base chakra in the form of a bubbling bowl, gently curving – a container in which the energies could be deeply embodied. It felt lovely.

The deep, rich stillness intensified and rooted more firmly as I continued to invite the energies of Ilahinoor to land within me. There was an unmistakable sensation of their presence, and I knew that they would always be there, for they were part of me. It was clear that they would also be able to be transmitted.

I was pulled very deep within as the energies took root, and I stayed immobile in a deep, rich space for a long time. The energies went down the legs and into the feet, where I felt them take residence. It felt as though the deepest grounding of Ilahinoor would fully manifest over time.

As all of this occurred, a strong sense of the Middle East was present. I felt a sense of oneness with the land, the people, and the ancientness of it all. The image of figures wearing long robes and walking on the Earth barefoot arose, along with a quiet, subtle yearning for, or maybe a remembrance of, this way of being. Perhaps the energies of Ilahinoor somehow carry this template of the human experience.

Since the energy of Ilahinoor went down the left side during my first experience, I was curious about what might happen with a second transmission, so I asked Kiara to send Ilahinoor to me again a week later. This time it went straight to the area around the right eye where a serious case of shingles had occurred a *few years before. The energies rooted around in there for quite some time, and the sense was that Ilahinoor was enhancing the ongoing healing process in that area of my being. The sensations eventually subsided, and I felt the experience was complete.*

Ilahinoor immediately felt like a breakthrough and a next step. Our initial experiences indicated that the energy contained the same level of transformational power as the Deeksha, with different and complementary effects. As with the Deeksha, we felt Ilahinoor altering our brain physiology, and sensed that repeated transmissions would result in the decommissioning of the ego-mind. Whereas the Deeksha strongly stimulated the upper chakras, Ilahinoor went deeper, grounding the higher energies within the lower chakras.

The Source of All had fulfilled the request for another, potentially more effective, means of catalyzing the collective awakening. We envisioned people passing Ilahinoor on to their family members, friends, and everyone who wanted to receive the transmission. Each one they touched could immediately share it with many others. In this way, the transmission would soon circle the globe with its blessings.

Sharing Ilahinoor

Our experiences of Ilahinoor prompted us to introduce the new transmission into our groups right away. After sharing Ilahinoor with an on-going group in Eugene, Oregon, we returned the following month to hear that those who had experimented with Ilahinoor had found its nature to be very feminine and deeply healing. Some felt the transmission deepening and grounding the openings in consciousness that had occurred through the Deeksha. Many experienced the divine light glowing more brightly within their physical forms. Nearly everyone reported that they found it easy and natural to call in Ilahinoor, feel its gentle, nourishing presence within them, and share the transmission with others. This feedback confirmed our own experiences with Ilahinoor, but the best was yet to come.

A new, very joyful face beamed out from among the group members. DeeDee had driven from her home an hour away to share her experiences with the group. She revealed that for years, a debilitating case of Lyme disease had severely limited her ability to move freely, making her full-time massage practice nearly impossible to continue. After she received Ilahinoor from a member of the Eugene group, she said, "I fell deeply asleep and when I awoke I felt refreshed and very alive and alert for the first time in two years."

Strongly intuiting that Ilahinoor could really help her, DeeDee soon shared the transmission with her friend, Til. DeeDee asked if Til would be willing to give Ilahinoor to her as often as possible for a few weeks. Til happily obliged.

After almost a month of near-daily transmissions, DeeDee found herself miraculously set free from the pain and immobility that had curtailed her activity. As her formerly intermittent sleep became deep and long, she felt rested for the first time in years. She resumed taking long walks and hikes and eventually began to cross-country ski again. As her energy increased, her bodywork practice was once again infused with ease and joy.

DeeDee's story deeply affected everyone in the room. We knew for sure that the Ilahinoor transmission could be passed on — and to great effect. Furthermore, DeeDee had begun to share Ilahinoor with her bodywork clients, finding it soothing and comforting to those recovering from stress and trauma. Some of them were likely passing Ilahinoor on to their friends and family. The transmission was already on its way around the world!

Before hearing DeeDee's account, we had some sense of the nurturing effects of Ilahinoor. But we had not anticipated that the transmission could precipitate such profound physical healing. DeeDee's story galvanized our commitment to sharing Ilahinoor whenever possible.

As people began to hear about Ilahinoor, we received emails from all over the globe asking us to share it with them. To expedite this effort, we began to offer teleconferences. What a joy to share this wonderful transmission with people all around the planet! As they shared their experiences with Ilahinoor during subsequent calls, we learned more about its healing blessings. Mental, emotional, and physical conditions, many of which had eluded other therapeutic approaches, were brought to the surface rapidly and gently for healing.

Reports continued to flow in, many of which can be found on our website. Here is a sample from an email:

I transmitted Ilahinoor to my daughter, who definitely has an active, stressed-filled, and ungrounded life at this time. She told me that she felt movement from the left side of her rib cage and under and around her heart, like when you hold a slinky in your hands and move it back and forth from one hand to the other. It was beautiful, she said.

Since that time she does feel more grounded and is handling the difficulties in her life with a quietness and calm that transcends what she ever dreamed of. She is so very grateful, and knows that what she is feeling is radiating to those in her immediate family.

I don't want this to sound like some kind of "high" that I'm on or that I've been converted to something – it is all very surreal, grounding, joyful, and nurturing... I am so grateful to both

of you and Kiara and those who help you for bringing in this
energy of Divine Light and passing it along to others, allowing
"us" too to pass it along.

Going Deeper with Ilahinoor

As we continued to share the new transmission, we found that
Ilahinoor delivered the divine light in a way that was very different from the Deeksha or meditation practices that access the
transcendental realms. Although many people experienced illuminations, the light did not remain in the head centers, but rather
penetrated deep within the body. The embodied nature of the
transmission prompted us to refer to Ilahinoor as the Divine Light
of the Goddess, for its energy is often experienced as deeply
feminine — soft and gentle, yet pervasive and powerful.

Experiencing and sharing Ilahinoor over time carried us ever more
deep into the subtle, mysterious realm of the Divine Feminine. We
were reminded of the twofold nature of the awakening process,
which embraces both the masculine and feminine qualities of Life
itself. Ilahinoor not only infused people with the bright white light
of the masculine, pouring in from above, but it also immersed them
into the rich, deep darkness of the feminine realms. This velvety,
fertile darkness magnetizes the white light of spirit into the physical body, enfolding it and giving it form and substance.

Within the realm of the divine feminine, we encounter the "dark
light"— the luminescence within form itself. We have all seen
this luminous darkness shining out from pupils of deepest black
in eyes that are alive to spirit. As the dark light of the depths
and the white light from above unify within us, the clear light
of consciousness shines forth. In this unity, we are able to *live*
our realizations; they weave into the very fabric of our being,
instead of flashing by as momentary glimpses of truth.

Awakening occurs when the *ida* and *pingala* nadis, which carry dark and white light respectively, come into balance. These two nadis transmit the primal yin and yang energy~consciousness up the spine, spiraling like a caduceus; at each point where they cross one another, a chakra coalesces. As the ida and pingala nadis progressively balance and activate, the central channel, or *sushumna nadi*, carries the Kundalini up from the base of the spine to energize each chakra and eventually to shower out the top of the head in a fountain of energy.

The bright white light so often looked for by spiritual seekers is only half of the equation; without the dark light, awakening cannot be complete or embodied. We are composed of both white and dark light endlessly blending and merging, as the yin-yang symbol illustrates. As human beings, we are each a bridge between the transcendental domains of spirit and the immanent realms of matter and form. When it integrates within us, the energy~consciousness of Ilahinoor can catalyze a deeply embodied experience of the fundamental unity of the divine masculine and feminine forces. We may perceive our very cells lighting up with radiance, held within the deep, dark womb-like matrix of the Mother.

Deep within the belly, just below the navel, lies the soul center, known variously as the *hara* or *tan tien*, the cosmic womb or egg, the abode of *shakti*, and the seat of the feminine or mother aspect of God. From this soul center emanates all manifest forms of life. Although Ilahinoor impacts all the chakras and soul centers, in many people it primarily focuses in the belly soul center. As it descends into the material realms as we can open ourselves, Ilahinoor brings the divine light of spirit as deep into the material realms as they can open to receive and enfold it. Ilahinoor also supports the process of sinking into the dark light of the divine feminine, the endlessly flowing fountain of Life, which nurtures and supports all living beings.

As this aspect of Self awakens no less than the transcendental realms, our very bodies are seen as sacred — fully divine, no less God than the transcendental realms of spirit. Perception of the matter worlds as maya or illusion dissolves in the full opening of the hara center. One's body is seen as a manifestation of Self, and all forms, all "other" bodies, are perceived as part of the Self. This manifestation might be expressed as *I AM One with the sacred womb of the Mother, birthing and holding all life in all universes.*

The image of the Egyptian Goddess Nut bending over the cosmos, enfolding it all in her vastness, illustrates this level of realization of Self. Ammachi, the hugging saint and avatar of south India, often says that all she wants to do is embrace as many of her children as possible while she is here. Her embodiment of the Divine Mother energy~consciousness is so complete that she views every single human being as one of her children.

Ilahinoor awakens the realization of embodied divinity and our oneness with all of Life. This transmission reveals the unified consciousness of life itself — the innate, omniscient, omnipresent illumination that pervades all of Creation. The primary purpose of this intelligence is to further life, to see every form of being flourish and to become more abundant. Here is how one woman expressed this purpose:

To me, Ilahinoor has a dark light, moist inner earth/plant vibrating quality that feels ideal for growing. The plant kingdom called to me after being introduced to Ilahinoor, too.... Even lumber on the side of a store under construction communicated.

As Ilahinoor enhances our awareness of the belly soul center, our ability to perceive this unity grows, and we begin to see it at work everywhere — within and without. Walking through a forest, we marvel at the symbiosis of the plants and animals living there.

Watching a bee gather pollen for its hive, we become aware that it simultaneously pollinates the plants it visits, enabling them to flower, bear fruit, and reproduce. We marvel at the innate intelligence that causes migratory birds to know when to fly south for the winter, and the unerring guidance system that leads them to their destination. The instant reaction that prompts us to flee in the face of danger, to cuddle and stroke a frightened baby, to eat when our energy dips, to sleep when the body needs rest — all are manifestations of the intelligence of Life.

We are born with this inner knowing at the core of our embodied being, our natural soul. It does not always remain accessible, though; psychoemotional traumas can diminish our communion with it. As we judge, deny, and separate from aspects of the psyche, and thus lose touch with the innate intelligence within us, addictions and other life-destroying behaviors arise. We can restore the psyche's wholeness by recovering these wounded aspects and bringing them back into conscious union with the soul. This restoration can occur when Ilahinoor is received over time in a setting supportive of healing and integrating what has not yet been loved and enfolded within our wholeness. In men and women alike, Ilahinoor not only impacts the brain/mind, but is also strongly experienced from the heart down, helping us to embrace the lower chakras and whatever they are holding that is now ready to be embraced and included in our totality.

It is important to remember that Ilahinoor cannot give us anything we do not already possess in latent form. The transmission activates our awareness of a dimension of our soul that is always awaiting discovery and unfoldment. The divine light of the One illuminates even the smallest atoms and molecules of our beingness; if it did not, they could not function. In fact, without the divine light, they, and we, would not be alive.

As Ilahinoor supports the light of our Infinite Source to burn more brightly within us, our presence in this world becomes ever more radiant. We become capable of igniting the divine spark in others through our mere presence, and through the expressions of the essence that emanate from us. Ilahinoor helps all that we bring forth — from writings, songs, and paintings to gardens and serene environments — to shine with the light of the One.

How People Experience Ilahinoor

Ilahinoor is most often experienced as a soothing, nurturing infusion or activation of light that is easily assimilable by virtually everyone. This soft, descending energy often feels like gentle waves moving through various parts of the body, down into the abdomen, pelvis, and sometimes into the legs and feet. It brings a deep sense of relaxation, a peace within the body that makes one feel comfortable and at home within it.

Ilahinoor assists those with active, stressed-filled lives to drop back into the body and reconnect with the natural rhythms and intelligence of Life. People who tend to feel ungrounded or "spacy" find that Ilahinoor helps them get back in touch with their innate sense of earthy, organic flow, and grounding. It is particularly helpful for those who spend a great deal of time in the mental realms.

Many who have received the Ilahinoor transmission report healings on all levels of being: spiritual, mental, emotional, and physical. Some healings are relatively minor, whereas others, like DeeDee's experience, border on the miraculous. People often find that distinctions between the various levels of being dissolve in awareness of the unity that Ilahinoor imparts. Similarly, its healing benefits are often experienced in a holistic way that transcends categorizations and permeates the entire being.

Of course, no one can know what, if any, direct healing will occur after an Ilahinoor transmission, and it is important to remember that Ilahinoor doesn't do the healing or create the results. Through grace, Ilahinoor assists in restoring awareness of the preexisting wholeness and integrity that have been obscured in consciousness. Although healing can and does occur, no one knows what the soul of each person is meant to experience as part of the divine plan for their unfoldment. As with all modalities and transmissions, Ilahinoor will go where it is needed and do what is most beneficial for its recipient and all involved.

Ilahinoor provides a foundational energy to support the awakening process, as it assists in healing and making whole the human psyche and natural soul. Without this foundation, even the most exalted spiritual energies have no place to land and be expressed. As the higher energies pour in, they tend to amplify any distortions in the psyche, which can exacerbate their symptoms and manifestations. Because it works to unify all of the life intelligence in the body, Ilahinoor can help in reuniting split-off aspects of the psyche with the soul.

Transforming separation into inclusivity and oneness is the underlying dynamic that promotes all healing. If, as we travel along the spiritual path, we continually focus on the purification, healing, and wholing of our humanness, we are far more likely to experience our divinity as fully embodied and eminently livable, active, and effective in the world. A life of joy, happiness, and fulfillment is more apt to take root and flower when we have provided the tender plant of our beingness with plenty of rich, moist compost, in addition to light, water, and fresh air.

If we have held spiritual judgments of ourselves, Ilahinoor can help us to relax these impossibly high standards and refrain from comparing ourselves to others. A woman who attended many Ilahinoor calls reported:

Usually spiritually exciting things don't happen to me, but when I just think of Ilahinoor my tummy heats up, especially right before I sleep. I also feel such peace and love inside I want to pinch myself to see if it's real.

I feel so close to the plants. I feel one with them. I always loved my garden and now the feeling has deepened into a joy even greater than before.

This woman went on to infuse her gardens with Ilahinoor so they would bless all who passed by with comfort and peace. She felt delighted with this simple, natural contribution to her neighborhood.

Disconnection with the innate intelligence of our human soul results in the ubiquitous *dis*eases of our times. Addictions, for example, indicate we have lost touch with what truly nourishes us, as does our attraction to eating and drinking things that harm the body. Overuse of stimulants such as sugar and caffeine, too, reflects a basic disconnection from our belly wisdom, as do emotional issues including fear of intimacy and codependence.

Ilahinoor is particularly helpful for those who feel lost and out of touch with their human self. If pressing issues involving relationships, home, family, and money are present, the lower chakras and belly soul center are probably in need of greater awareness. When people accumulate an excess of unintegrated higher energies — for instance, from meditating for hours a day — they are often flooded with an immediate sense of relief as the Ilahinoor transmission helps the rarefied frequencies descend and land. As the lower chakras are bathed in the high light, allowing consciousness openings to be integrated and embodied, the subtle body and chakra systems come back into balance.

An overcharge in the upper chakras may impart transcendent bliss and a sense of rising above the difficult feelings and issues of the world. However pleasurable this experience may be, it is almost always a temporary state that will be followed by an equally strong descent. As Taoist philosophy teaches, life continuously moves from one polarity to its opposite, seeking balance. Staying connected to the hara center and the lower chakras, and experiencing Ilahinoor on a regular basis can help us to welcome the descent rather than to experience it as a painful crash. In fact, Ilahinoor reminds us that each ascent into the higher realms must be followed by a corresponding deepening and integration period, if it is to be fully embodied and lived.

Ilahinoor may bring to the surface feelings and memories that have not yet been fully faced and felt. It shines attention on the belly soul center, and whatever has been held there is now ready to be seen, felt, and accepted more deeply. When such material arises, we suggest reminding yourself that facing and embracing it is an integral aspect of awakening. You can invite the breath into the belly, and feel it penetrating right into the core of the sensation or feeling there. As you fully feel it, remember to release it just as fully on the outbreath. Turn it over to the One who knows how best to bring it all into healing and wholeness. Rest in the arms of Divine Mother as She comforts you through the emotional storm. Feel Her sustaining love and caring enfolding you. Listen as She whispers the messages that She alone can give you.

A woman who received Ilahinoor described her experience of this process:

This morning I thought about Ilahinoor and called that energy in. The most beautiful, loving energy filled me. It was so gentle. It allowed me to embrace more of my pain and let it move through me. I cried for joy, for the whole thing. My vision feels different. It's like I can see more of what's love peeking through what goes on out here. I'm ecstatic in the mellowest sort of way.

Contagious Ease

As we continued to share Ilahinoor in person and through tele-conferences, reports of the changes people were experiencing poured in. Many found that working with Ilahinoor made facing their remaining unintegrated emotional content easier. As the belly soul center flowered, resistance to the more challenging aspects of awakening faded away. "I never knew it could be so easy to feel things — even the things I thought would be the hardest — and let them go," became a common refrain, as a European woman expressed after a teleconference:

I experienced a wonderful sense of lightness and groundedness, very in my body, and the miracle was that although it was very cathartic, it was not ungrounded in any way, and I never felt over-whelmed, which was great.

In fact, I felt after a few hours quite liberated, in that I felt in touch with myself and very authentic, which I have not felt in a long time — a sense of being able to not only feel my feelings, but express them! So it helped me to feel grounded enough to express my feelings!

Truly liberating, and, in essence, therapeutic. It is a wonderful energy.

Ilahinoor helps us to be present with What Is, within and without. Saying "No" to what is present in our mental-emotional world not only comes between us and our experience, but it also postpones our awareness of the true Self. When we can say "Yes" to whatever arises, we are one with the soul, our inner divinity, which accepts and embraces everything, without exception.

In our groups, we noticed that the more comfortable people became with facing and embracing whatever was present, the more gently and tenderly they treated themselves and one another. *We are one*, they seemed to be seeing, even in our unhealed emotions.

We all have the same "stuff" – the greed, envy, anger, and sadness, the yearning to be free. The story may differ, but the underlying feelings are the same.

After receiving Ilahinoor, many people reported a new sense of inner quietness and peace, and a relaxation into and acceptance of themselves, their lives, and their awakening process. Some saw that struggle only occurs when we resist what is present and think that something different should be happening. The actual emotional content was not so hard to face, they realized; the judgment that it was wrong or bad to feel what they were feeling had filled the process with conflict.

Suffering had been compounded by spiritual beliefs such as *I should be beyond this emotion. If I were truly awake, none of this would be present. I need to hide these feelings and pretend that everything is calm and clear.* As Ilahinoor opened up an allowing space for everything that was present, these judgments were replaced by greater self-acceptance and equanimity. Emotional tempests might continue to rise and fall, but deep within was a place that could contain them all and allow them to pass through, without the damage that might have previously occurred from holding back and then venting strong feelings.

After receiving Ilahinoor, daily life flowed more smoothly for many, as they discovered great joy in the everyday tasks that had once seemed boring, meaningless, or irrelevant to what they had thought awakening was all about. Feeling isolated and alone in a separate little bubble gave way to a palpable sense of unity with all forms of life, from trees and rocks to the birds out in the yard.

We were especially happy to hear from those who had become imbalanced from too many highlight activations, without enough corresponding attention paid to the embodiment of vaster energies and transmissions. A Scandinavian man's email described his feelings of despondency after months of finding himself lost and adrift. The many Deekshas Erik had received had apparently dismantled his sense of self so thoroughly that he no longer had a clear sense of the meaning of his life. After his first experience of Ilahinoor, he wrote:

It feels very wonderful to see and feel the changes that happen with Ilahinoor. It is like a gentle mother coming and comforting and showing everything is going to be all right.

Erik's depression lifted and he went on to share the blessings he had received from Ilahinoor with others in similar situations.

A woman who found Ilahinoor so resonant she went on to join nearly every teleconference we offered had this to say after her first experience of the energies:

Since the transmission, the refrain I-laaaaa-hee-noor has moved through me spontaneously accompanied with the downflow of a wide stream of bright liquid light that enters the crown, zips down to the belly, splits down the legs and out the soles into tiny light-filled roots. Quite amazing. The energy feels so right/needed/ good/balancing.

The Ilahinoor energy feels to me like that complete relaxation that occurs when falling into a big soft chair after a long hard day. The chair provides deep rest and support as I realize I didn't know how tired and out-of-balance I was. Or how a long drink of fresh water tastes after not realizing how thirsty I actually had become. Ilahinoor really does enliven.

If there is one thing Ilahinoor seems to impart to the human self, it is this sense of being at home in our own skin. As we sink into flowing more easily with the rhythms of Life, we find ourselves responding to whatever comes with the carefree abandon of a child playing in a sandbox. As it continues to be passed from person to person, circling the globe, Ilahinoor helps the focus of humanity's attention to shift from contagious disease to contagious ease. What a joy to envision a world full of people happy to be themselves, just as they are!

Ilahinoor in Addiction Recovery

After receiving Ilahinoor during a teleconference, a physician began to share the transmission with recovering addicts in a rehabilitation facility that, up until then, had not been a calm and peaceful place. Here is Dr. R's description of what ensued when he asked Ilahinoor to touch each of the patients:

There was an immediate visible change. The normal addict negativism lifted. There was a feeling of lightness and almost joy.

The next day, all forty transmitted Ilahinoor to each other. All I could do was break down in tears. Then, on Family Day, one hundred people gave the energy to each other. The same thing happened. The entire Universe stopped — was in between breaths — nothing and everything at the same time. It makes me weep with tears of joy.

Conflicts have been reduced by 75%, and this is the week of the full moon. Everything was so peaceful; everyone went around the grounds in silence, like monks in a cloister.

Eighteen people are in detox now, and usually they go through excruciating pain. They still have pain, but they were almost peacefully transitioning. The detox usually takes a few days, and it took a few hours!

We don't touch each other at the house. All of this was done by sending Ilahinoor with intention and by name. As everyone joined in chanting "I-la-hi-noor," it just went where it wanted to go, in waves. It is such a beautiful sound, to hear one hundred people chanting — the vibration is tremendous. Then this holy hush comes over them.

During calls, when Dr. R described the "holy hush," it came over us all. He later met with an imam who emphasized the extreme sacredness of the word Ilahinoor. "When we speak the word, we are raising the light of God within us," Dr. R explained.

In light of Dr. R's experiences at the rehab center, the potential for similar benefits with other types of addiction — eating disorders, caffeine and nicotine addiction, and all other forms of seeking without what can only be found within — immediately comes to mind. A vast realm of possibility lies as yet unexplored, just waiting for those who feel called to participate in a grand experiment.

Endless Opportunities to Experience Ilahinoor

As teleconferences brought together people living all across the globe, we all delighted in hearing how others were sharing the Ilahinoor transmission — not only with other humans, but also with animals, birds, trees, and places. A man named Skandar uplifted us all as he described sharing Ilahinoor with the beings and places he encountered in his journey through life. After transmitting Ilahinoor to some bristlecone pine trees, for instance, Skandar pointed out that because all members of a particular tree species are part of one group soul, they could share Ilahinoor with one another after he'd transmitted it to them. With his extraordinary sensitivity to the life in all forms, Skandar felt this joyful sharing taking place.

Skandar inspired the two of us to go out into our yard and transmit Ilahinoor to the juniper trees there. As we tuned in to them, we felt the deep sadness in these sylvan beings for being so little valued in the area where we live. Viewing them as water-guzzlers, farmers and ranchers cut down large swaths of junipers, oblivious not only to their vital role in the hydrological cycle that provides basic sustenance to us all, but also to their inherent sacredness as living beings. The junipers seemed to drink in Ilahinoor, and we sensed they were grateful for the rare gift of being seen as a valuable part of Creation. Taking our cue from Skandar, we asked them to share Ilahinoor with all other junipers, and to convey that they are loved by at least two members of the species that seemed intent on eradicating them from Earth.

Skandar also often shared Ilahinoor with injured raptors in a rehab center near his home. Sometimes, he reported that Ilahinoor aided them in their healing process, and described the exhilaration of watching as a bird was set free. At other moments, Skandar felt Ilahinoor ease the transition out of the body for those too injured to survive.

Before sharing Ilahinoor with nonhuman beings, Skandar always checked in with them to be sure they were receptive to the energies. If he didn't feel an unqualified "Yes," he didn't transmit Ilahinoor to them. He also tuned in to determine when a transmission was complete, and how frequently to share Ilahinoor with each recipient. Animals and birds, he said, often communicated through eye contact and subtle movements that let Skandar know when the being had received enough energy for the time being. With trees, other plants, rocks, and land masses, Skandar's highly developed intuition indicated when a transmission was appropriate, the most effective way to deliver it, and when it felt complete.

Hearing Skandar's many accounts of sharing Ilahinoor prompted us to ask to be conduits for Ilahinoor to pour through and permeate the atmosphere in a variety of public spaces, from large stores to airports. Whenever we found ourselves in such a place, we'd make ourselves available to being utilized by the Divine in this way. We'd also ask that all who were ready to receive the grace of Ilahinoor be blessed by it as they passed through the space, in exactly the right way for each soul.

Calling in Ilahinoor particularly eased the challenges often encountered in modern travel. In a train, we'd ask that Ilahinoor fill our compartment, and then all the cars. This seemed to make the impersonal space more friendly and harmonious. On an airplane, if the pilot announced there would be turbulence ahead, we'd send Ilahinoor out in front of the plane. More often than not, it smoothed the way for us all to travel onward in comfort.

Here is how one woman described the ways Ilahinoor was weaving itself into the fabric of her daily life:

lahinoor is chanting itself through me even when I don't call it forth – in Home Depot, in the midst of traffic jams. It's singing itself into situations where it wants to be.

The Grace of Ilahinoor

Everyone who receives Ilahinoor can immediately pass it on to anyone else who would like to experience it. Some people may require a few transmissions to lock into the source of the energies and feel their frequencies coming alive within them; but with repeated exposure Ilahinoor makes itself known in a palpable way. Even when bodily sensations or consciousness shifts seem elusive, people find that experiencing Ilahinoor over time subtly, yet noticeably, alters their experience of life.

The process of integrating Ilahinoor can resemble that of growing a garden. After the first few transmissions of Ilahinoor, the seeds have been planted, but we may not see the tender, green shoots peeking above the ground for some time to come. If we return to the garden two or three month later, the emergence of new life becomes obvious. Then, we might recognize the ways in which Ilahinoor has fine-tuned our perception and increased our sense of the underlying unity beneath the apparently separate forms we each inhabit.

As the fabric of our being is rewoven and integrated with the spiritual dimensions of consciousness, our awareness of that which supports life increases. Many people who work with Ilahinoor over time find themselves making dietary changes, embarking on cleansing programs, and, in general, focusing on more fully nurturing the human form as a vessel for the soul and spirit. It is common to shift from an excessively linear, goal-driven, masculine orientation to a way of being that incorporates feminine wisdom and reverence for life. This shift can mean more sleep, rest, and quiet contemplation — the hallmarks of a balanced existence that are often devalued in the busy modern world.

Receiving Ilahinoor heightens the evolutionary process already underway in each of us, but even more evolution is catalyzed as we transmit the energies to others. Stepping into sharing the Ilahinoor transmission brings about a major leveling, especially in those who have believed some sort of spiritual pedigree was required to access the Divine. A radical shift in identity occurs as we realize we are capable of inviting sacred energies to pour through us to bless others.

Some of the most touching moments we've experienced in sharing Ilahinoor have occured as rooms full of people take turns giving and receiving Ilahinoor. The rich, sacred silence that permeates the room, the radiant glow emanating from all present, and the loving oneness that unites everyone attest to the majesty that lives within us all, just waiting to come forth and be shared. As Ilahinoor pours through all alike — the shy and self-doubting as well as the confident and fearless — we see one another in our true identity as representatives of the Divine here on Earth.

When we directly experience divine energies being activated within us and flowing through us from the Source, there is no question that we are one with God. Further, when we place our hands on another and witness him/her lighting up with divine energy, the reality that we are also capable of transferring blessing-grace becomes self-evident. This realization bypasses deeply embedded beliefs of our limitations and all the stories about our separation, sin, and unworthiness that have been held in the collective unconscious for millennia. In sharing Ilahinoor, the truth is revealed through direct demonstration. Can there be anything more satisfying than stepping into our divine birthright?

Because it has no rules or limits, no long training programs, no hierarchies of influence or organizational structures, Ilahinoor is available to all. People are free to share Ilahinoor with friends, co-workers, church members, animals, pets, plants, trees, and birds. Anyone can ask to be a conduit for Ilahinoor to fill a building, a bus, an area of a city, a nation, or whole regions of the world that might benefit from its soothing, healing, vibrational frequencies. When we hear of a disaster anywhere on the planet, we can immediately ask to be a conduit for Ilahinoor to flow through us to that area and all its inhabitants. And, of course, it is a great joy to envision the entire planet and everyone on it bathed in the healing, nurturing grace of Ilahinoor.

Reading about Ilahinoor opens the mind to new possibilities and prepares the way for the living reality of Ilahinoor to reveal itself to you. Experiencing Ilahinoor is far more catalytic, for it has the potential to activate your awareness of new dimensions of your being, and of life itself. The way to find out about those dimensions is through your own personal exploration. Because nothing impacts consciousness more than our own direct experience, we offer the following experiential immersion into the frequencies of Ilahinoor.

Experience~Activation: Ilahinoor

Find a quiet, comfortable place in which you can remain for a time. At first, you will be sitting, and later it will be best to lie down.

As you sit quietly, allow your eyes to close and become aware of your breathing. Feel the breath coming into the body and then going back out. Letting your awareness sink into the breath, feel yourself traveling into the inner world.

Invite the breath into any physical or emotional sensation that is present. Feel it, and then, on the outbreath, let it flow through you back into the totality of Life. Continue feeling and releasing, breath by breath. In this way, you are breathing open a space into which you can invite Ilahinoor when it is time for that to occur.

Contemplate all that you have read about Ilahinoor. What deeply spoke to you about this transmission? What does it offer that would be food for your soul? How might Ilahinoor offer sustenance to your human self in its journey of awakening? Allow a few minutes to consider these questions.

Now, feel how much you would like to directly experience the blessing of Ilahinoor. From the sacred space in your heart of hearts, call to the One Divine Presence out of which all emanates:

I open myself now to experience the grace of Ilahinoor. I am ready to receive it now!

Chanting the sacred word Ilahinoor three times aloud is a powerful way to open the channels for the grace of Ilahinoor to pour in. The word Ilahinoor is composed of two root syllables: ilah, which refers to the Divine, and noor, which means light. To pronounce Ilahinoor, divide it into four syllables as follows:

EE

LAH'

HEE

NOOR

Ilahinoor is an extremely sacred word in the Islamic tradition. Feel the magnificence and grandeur of the word and its meaning as you chant it aloud. Know that giving voice to the word literally calls in the Light of our Infinite Source, and raises the divine light that already lives within each of us.

After you have chanted or spoken the word Ilahinoor aloud three times, feel yourself opening like a flower to receive the transmission. You may feel it pouring down from above, or coming alive within you, or both. Feel the transmission going wherever it is most needed. Welcome Ilahinoor into the belly soul center, if it wants to go there. Allow plenty of time for Ilahinoor to do whatever it seems to want to do within you, until the process feels complete.

Then invite Ilahinoor to flow into your arms and settle into your hands, awakening your ability to transmit Ilahinoor to others. Let this take as long as it likes, until you feel confident that you can share Ilahinoor with anyone who would like to receive it.

When the sitting portion of the transmission seems to be complete, and you feel the frequencies of Ilahinoor alive within you, lie down and allow the transmission to continue to deepen and integrate on all levels of your being. Allow plenty of time for this part of the process. Many people find fifteen to thirty minutes to be helpful.

After this act feels complete, ask to be shown anything else that will help Ilahinoor deepen in you. A glass of water, a walk in nature, or connecting with a beloved pet are some ways this transmission may want to be assisted into a richer, fuller level of integration.

Be gentle with yourself after the transmission has landed within you. Resist the temptation to get busy; allow the grace of Ilahinoor to continue to settle in over time. And, remember that whenever you like, you can once again call in the blessing-grace of Ilahinoor.

Ilahinoor: An Evolutionary Gift of Grace

In the bigger picture, the spread of Ilahinoor is occurring as an answer to an evolutionary need. The Earth and humanity are ascending into a new dimension of existence. The very fabric of matter/energy that forms the basis of our physical experience is shifting octaves, birthing a new, higher-dimensional species and planet.

Ilahinoor ignites the light of Source in the very heart of matter, the light within all form. When it becomes sufficiently illumined and awakened, matter goes through a phase shift analogous to what happens when water melts from ice into a liquid, and then, with a sufficient energy increase, into an invisible gas. A similar upleveling is occurring with your body and the planet as you read this.

Ilahinoor offers a gift of grace that allows this upleveling to take place in a more harmonious and expeditious manner. In its infinite love, the Divine wants to make this shift as easy as possible for all of us. The grace of Ilahinoor seems to soften the journey, smoothing out the rough patches and reminding us to nurture ourselves, one another, and all of life every step of the way.

There are many ways of describing this massive evolutionary shift that is now underway. The two of us like to refer to it as the birthing of the Luminous Self. We are graduating from thinking of ourselves as a small, limited self, to realizing that we are actually a vast, magnificent, radiant Self. As our fundamental sense of identity shifts away from the separation and unconsciousness of the human condition, our self-sense reorients to center within the unified, limitless luminosity of our true nature. Because it helps us to become aware of the Divine Light that we are, and to directly experience the radiance that lives within every cell of our being, Ilahinoor is of great assistance in the process of birthing the Luminous Self.

As we come to know ourselves as radiant beings of light, and as that light embodies more and more deeply within us, Ilahinoor may continue to catalyze our evolution as souls in the human experience. For the two of us, working deeply with Ilahinoor over many months opened a door that led to receiving two other transmissions of Grace that we call Love~Oneness and Spotless Mind. Each of the three transmissions activates a specific soul center and arena of experience. When combined and experienced over time, all three contribute to a balanced awakening process that eventuates in the realization that we are each a Luminous Self, here to radiate our frequencies into an awakening world.

We share all three transmissions through teleconferences and in-person groups and events. For information on our schedule as well as much more about all three Transmissions of Grace, we welcome you to visit our website, LuminousSelf.com. There, you will find specific information on how we transmit Ilahinoor to others, both in person and at a distance, practical guidelines, and legal and ethical considerations. You can also read many more accounts of how people have experienced Ilahinoor and the other transmissions we share.

Ilahinoor and the other Transmissions of Grace feature prominently in our book, *Agents of Grace*, Part Two of the *Birthing the Luminous Self* trilogy. In *Agents of Grace*, we describe the natural progression from awakening to the soul as our true identity (which is the theme of our first book, *Soul Awakening*), to activating the ability to serve as a conduit of grace. We share what we have learned and experienced with Ilahinoor and the other Transmissions of Grace, how the three transmissions harmonize and complement one another, and the ways they contribute to a balanced, grounded awakening process. For more information on *Agents of Grace* and our other books, please see our website.

chapter 26

Embodying
Divine Light

by Sarah Godwin

Sarah and her husband, David, have been working with Ilahinoor since 2008. At the time of writing, they were leading workshops in the UK, Poland, and Spain. Sarah's website is Ilahinoor.co.uk, *and she can be reached at* sarahg@Ilahinoor.co.uk.

---○---

Ilahinoor found me in 2007 when I read about it on Kiara's website. I was drawn to the idea that Ilahinoor could open the whole body to awakened consciousness, but it was the experience of a deeply soothing, loving energy in the days that followed that persuaded me to investigate it further.

I had been receiving Oneness Deeksha for a year or so, and had experienced some significant emotional clearing and shifts of consciousness; however, the opening I felt was primarily around the head and heart, and I was finding myself *spacing out* somewhat. I also knew of others who were having difficulty grounding and integrating the effects. The most profound shift, to my surprise, happened spontaneously during a family holiday in Spain, where I was nowhere near a live Deeksha giver but was reading a book about it. I underwent a powerful initiation, following which I felt the energy flowing out through me.

I felt somewhat crushed, on my return home, to be told that I could not possibly transmit Deeksha without undergoing the official process in India. I considered going to India to become an official Deeksha giver, but what I really wanted was to help people *embody* this awakening of consciousness.

I have always felt that spirituality should not be treated as separate from everyday life. It is too easy to get lost in high states of consciousness while losing our connection with the physical body and ordinary reality. This Ilahinoor transmission seemed to offer a more integrated approach, and promoted a direct connection with the Source; it made me curious to learn more.

Naturally skeptical, and despite the pull I felt, I was unsure of whether Kiara Windrider and his transmission were the genuine article. So I signed up for a retreat with him in the Swiss Alps — I reckoned that at the very least I would have a great holiday in the snow! But my doubts could not have been more unfounded; this retreat turned out to be the pivotal point of my entire life. Along with Deeksha, I had been using Reiki and other energy and deep body work for some years, and was familiar with deep levels of perception and altered states of consciousness, but Ilahinoor opened me very quickly to something quite new.

Three years on, it's sometimes hard to recall what it was like at the beginning, as this sense of vast inner spaciousness, together with a deep stability, quickly began to feel normal. When I introduce people to Ilahinoor for the first time and experience their wonder and gratitude, I recapture the magic of that retreat in Switzerland.

My response to the first hands-on transmission was rather dramatic. I experienced an immediate release of negative energy patterns through spontaneous body movements, and was then unable to speak or move for at least two hours. Thereafter, I discovered I would drop spontaneously into a quite unfamiliar state of consciousness whenever I relaxed, especially just before and after sleep — a very open, spacious state that felt as if I were swimming around an infinite universe inside of me. I was having mystical visions of ancient Egypt — something that I would never have expected — yet I was not disconnected from ordinary reality. I was

146

deep in this open, clear, and peaceful state but also very securely in the body, and connected with the physical environment. There was a deep heart connection with other people and with nature, and a lightness of being that didn't take anything too seriously.

Uncomfortable, even profoundly painful states arose at times, but I moved through them remarkably quickly. Receiving or giving myself the Ilahinoor transmission allowed me to fully embrace whatever I was feeling, and the contraction would release into something even more open than before.

This experience continues to be a pattern. After a great expansion, I often experience an Ilahinoor hangover for a day or so — a somewhat contracted and agitated state, generally with physical discomfort and negative thoughts. It has happened enough times now for me to trust that this feeling will usually last no more than a day, and is usually followed by a state of peaceful, connected ordinariness in which life flows with ease.

I realized during this first retreat with Kiara that everything I had done in my life so far was a preparation for this experience — I was excited to discover how beautifully my existing work with listening touch and deep body release harmonized with Ilahinoor, and had the sense that a new phase of life was beginning. I realized that I was the first person from the UK to attend one of Kiara's Ilahinoor seminars, and I was filled with a missionary enthusiasm to take this amazing transmission home and share it with as many people as possible. But I felt some trepidation; was I simply on a spiritual high that would dissolve when I left Kiara and this magical Alpine setting? Would Ilahinoor really cross the English Channel with me?

I gave my first transmission to a friend at home, and was surprised and relieved to discover that not only did Ilahinoor flow powerfully, but also when she gave it to me in return, it felt every bit as strong as it had in Switzerland. One of the greatest attributes of this energy is that it is simply available to anyone who is drawn to use it. Although it was certainly a profound experience to spend ten days on retreat with Kiara, clearly not everyone must undergo such a formal process.

I had come home with my mission of immediately launching Ilahinoor in a big way, but that is not what actually happened. I didn't have the immediate response I had hoped for, which left me feeling somewhat flat and disappointed. What did happen, however, was some very sweet and intense work with just two or three close friends, and some deep healing for myself. Eventually, I let go of needing to make anything happen, and at that exact point people started to appear, through apparent coincidences, who were very interested in Ilahinoor, and the work started to take off effortlessly.

From this experience I learned two important things: firstly, that Ilahinoor, though gentle, is very powerful, and can initiate both a fast release of deeply entrenched limiting patterns, and an embodiment of high levels of new energy. Our deepest structures start to change, and although it is not necessary to be completely clear or healed in order to give Ilahinoor to others, we must give priority to our own process and allow ourselves the time and space to integrate these shifts.

The second understanding was that the appropriate people will be drawn to Ilahinoor at the appropriate time, and that I have to trust this process! I am always meeting people at our workshops who heard about it through some odd synchronicity, often at the last moment; who knew they had to come but didn't know why; who had felt something new was coming for a while, or who recognized Ilahinoor as an energy they had already been experiencing. I love that the more deeply Ilahinoor opens me to my true nature, the more accepting and trusting I become that this is how all of life works — if we can allow it!

I wrote the following three months after my return from Switzerland:

I am noticing not only shifts and expansions of perception, but also a distinct change in the nature of my body-consciousness. At the mental-emotional level, I am moving rapidly between states — from excitement to wobbly fear to joy to confusion. But all of these feelings are held within an expanding quality of profoundly secure embodiment.

For some years, through various dance, movement, and meditation practices, I have been entering more deeply into my body, becoming more at home in myself; but what I experience now is quite unprecedented. It is really hard to put into words, but I feel somehow more solid and rooted, and at the same time more spacious and filled with light. It is like a visceral experience of Divine love — God is my blood, my bones, my skin, my breath... and accessing this place of secure body-bliss is not dependent on how I am feeling physically or emotionally. I can, for example, have severe indigestion or a headache and the underlying state is unaffected, and in fact can be drawn upon to help me enter the pain with healing.

One of the most exciting effects during the first year or so of Ilahinoor was the opening of my inner vision. I must admit I had previously been quite skeptical both of so-called past life experiences and of the appearance of angels and Ascended Masters. But in addition to some wonderful psychedelic colored light shows, I was finding myself after Ilahinoor transmissions going into deep trance states in which various Egyptian scenarios were experienced, and I was visited by Babaji, Christ, the Buddha, and assorted angels!

The first time my husband. David, gave me Ilahinoor, we had an extraordinary mutual Egyptian experience. Following the transmission I went into an altered state, and after various Egyptian visions, found myself in a huge, dark smoky hall filled with people who were all bowing down before some kind of king or deity, clad in gold, who was sitting on a throne on a raised platform. I was so fully in this scenario that in deep awe and devotion I felt compelled to fall to the floor and prostrate myself at David's feet. The bit of me that was witnessing this vision felt rather foolish, but when David bent down and laid his hand on my head in blessing, I felt appropriately honored.

David, meanwhile, had felt himself change physically and grow very tall. He experienced himself to be some kind of god-like figure dressed in gold, up on a dais in a great dark hall in front of a vast crowd of prostrated worshippers. So when I fell to the ground in front of him, it was the most natural thing in the world to reach down and give me a blessing.

As you can imagine, David never lets me forget this. I should add that afterwards — and this is how life with Ilahinoor has become — we went and ate dinner in front of the TV with no sense of disconnection between the two experiences!

Another common experience, that I have heard reported by others, is a very physical sense of becoming one with the Earth. About three months after first receiving Ilahinoor, I wrote about a particularly powerful experience:

Being Gaia

Following an Ilahinoor session, I had a profound experience of embodied oneness. During the session, I had felt an exceptionally strong connection with Earth energy, with a powerful flow coming up through my feet. Afterward, bathed in the energy, I had the physical experience of my body becoming entirely enclosed by flesh — it felt blissfully safe and secure, luscious, soft, and warm. At first I wondered if I was back in the womb, but then I understood that this was a physical experience of oneness — all of humanity was literally one flesh.

As I rested in the sensation of expanded consciousness, I had a spherical awareness of this one body spread over the surface of the globe. Gradually, I began to incorporate all fleshly beings, then all forms of life, until I was the living skin of the world. I became Gaia, a single living organism with a pulsating core, not separate from the Universe.

This experience was not simply a vision or a concept, but a physical and sensate experience. This sense of being not just a personal body, but also somehow connected with the body of the Earth, remains with me now, underpinning everything.

It is interesting now, more than three years later, to read the above and recall the intensity of the first year or two with Ilahinoor. The profound healing and expansion of consciousness experienced by myself and others was thrilling. I was organizing seminars for Kiara, and David and I were also beginning to teach Ilahinoor around the country. Highlights included a trip to Egypt with Kiara and Grace (an extraordinary journey of initiation during which it really felt as if we had entered another dimension); connecting with elemental Earth energies in Ireland, and the intense degree of unconditional love I would feel when giving the transmission to a large group of people. I was experiencing a great expansion of potential, in terms of my capacity as an individual and as a human being.

Then something changed, and everything gradually began to appear somewhat flat. I was leading workshops where the participants were having profound experiences, but for me the visionary, multidimensional aspect was much diminished, and even when those experiences occurred, they seemed of less interest and importance. I was much more interested in doing ordinary practical things. Although the energetic quality of Ilahinoor by this time felt deeply embodied, the excitement and missionary zeal were gone.

There was disenchantment with what had so far been largely a journey of experience. I had achieved deep insights, profound visions, and amazing revelations, but had a sense that all of this enlightenment was not ultimately significant. I was lost and confused and entered a period of depression — something that I had hoped Ilahinoor had banished forever.

In this new, much less enjoyable place, I started to question the possibilities of Ilahinoor as the route to ultimate awakening but continued to use it both with others and myself. I was sharing it almost daily with a friend who was going through a very difficult activation of traumatic childhood experiences.

During this period, I gained a deeper understanding and respect for the healing nature of the transmission, and the depths to which it can take us when we commit deeply to Life. When we inquire into the nature of a pain, whether physical or emotional, we tend to arrive at a place where we naturally want to turn back. Something in our conditioning tells us that it is not safe to go any further. It can almost feel as if we will die if we pass this threshold.

What I have experienced is that Ilahinoor serves as a *chalice of love*, in which we are able to meet fully, embrace, and ultimately move through this pain into a place of great spaciousness. But despite all the experience of love and healing, this commitment to clearing our most deeply held patterns is not always an easy path, and often requires us to move away from what is safe and familiar toward the realm of the unknown.

"At a certain point," says the spiritual teacher Adyashanti, "your relationship with spirituality is going to turn from something that is based in experience, to the letting go and dissolution of self. You allow this falling away to happen. You don't do it, you don't know how to do it. All you have to do is allow it to happen."[1]

Easier said than done, as the mind tries every strategy it can muster to maintain control over a self that never really existed in the first place. Of course, as Kiara writes, this dissolution of identity is happening now, whether we choose it or not — but we are deeply conditioned to believe that we have to make things happen. Simply allowing something to unfold is one of the hardest things for us humans! Ilahinoor can open us to this space of allowing, of simply letting be, so that the movement of Life can flow without resistance.

During the winter of 2009, I went through a phase of working very intensively with the Merkaba activation, which promoted a great acceleration of letting go of mental control. After a few days of feeling almost suicidal, I experienced a subtle yet fundamental shift. There came a recognition of the complete futility of trying to control anything with the mind, and the focal point of my awareness seemed to turn around. Following this shift, there was a period when I seemed to be losing my grip on ordinary reality — I was either a ghost or in a world of ghosts. Ilahinoor, at this point, became a great stabilizer, and I could see clearly how it worked in support of the Merkaba activation.

The last year or so has been quite a rollercoaster ride, as old structures have fallen away to reveal for a while something very free, before another contraction grips and life obligingly throws up the perfect circumstances to challenge any reinflation of the ego. During this phase, Ilahinoor has continued to be my anchor and companion, still offering a loving yet unswerving process of opening, revealing, embracing, and dissolving.

When I feel stuck or confused or lost in the story, I make a little inner intention and say the name, which is how I make my connection with Ilahinoor, and eventually I am washed with loving presence and the sense of being soothingly held; the mind will quiet and clearing will happen.

I have found that working with movement, breath, and sound can allow a deeper, faster, and more complete clearing. After a year or so with Ilahinoor, I started to find this kinetic release happening quite spontaneously whenever any stress or negative emotion arose. When the system reaches a certain frequency, lower vibrations are no longer stored and embedded, they can spontaneously be released.

The more I work with Ilahinoor, the less I feel I will ever be able to offer any intellectually satisfying explanation of its nature. Because it takes us beyond third-dimensional consciousness, any attempt to define it feels like trying to wrestle an octopus into a box! My sense now is that Ilahinoor is not something I am given from beyond, but is simply an experience of coming home to what I already am.

If I look back to life before Ilahinoor, I can see what a profound shift there has been. All the usual stuff persists — internal arguments, judgments, conditioned responses — yet it all happens in an infinitely vast embracing space. My experience of life now is more like surfing a wave than struggling on a battlefield. I have stopped reaching for anything, stopped becoming fixated with cosmic experiences, and have started to embrace and celebrate the sacred ordinariness of life.

David and I often teach workshops in which we support Ilahinoor with craniosacral therapy, dance, and movement. After introducing Ilahinoor and its context, the emphasis is always on the experiences of the participants, and their exploration of what they encounter in themselves and each other, often through touch and movement.

When emotions come up, we always encourage people to let them unravel through the body. Some people find that release happens for them in deep stillness, others find that letting the body move spontaneously offers not only a fuller release, but also a new level of trust in their deeper innate wisdom.

I have been offering a process that is still evolving, and which begins with a transmission of Ilahinoor and opens into an exploration through movement, touch, and sound. I have experimented with starting out with the group sitting in a circle, leaning against each other back to back as we tune into Ilahinoor. I encourage them to become aware of small internal movements, and then feel if this experience wants to grow into something larger.

Participants may get up and start moving, whether alone or in contact with someone else, always with an awareness of their relationships with each other, the Earth, and the cosmos. Sounds may also arise, usually starting off as a cacophony of individual noises, but then weaving together into a beautiful and powerful group expression. I sometimes supply props — pieces of fabric, hats, scarves — that add a dimension for exploration and expression. A profound and exhilarating performance of spontaneous theatre can emerge, with potent energy greater than the sum of the individual participants.

This group alchemy is an important aspect of our gatherings. I always sense that the right people have synchronistically come together in the right place for some larger purpose. We can often feel how a particular group soul is interacting with the Earth, even though the purpose may be beyond our understanding.

This feeling was felt particularly strongly when we facilitated a group in a building on the site of the infamous Warsaw ghetto. We experienced the energy there as heavy and difficult, and found ourselves drawn to activate the Merkaba of the building and the area, and danced and sang around the courtyard in order not to be submerged by the heaviness. Most of the group went on to experience much joy and lightness for the remainder of that weekend, and some very deep healing took place.

The original message that came through in Turkey — and Kiara's personal intention — is that Ilahinoor is something that belongs to us all equally — not something to be trademarked or turned into a system. This understanding is demonstrated by Kiara's invitation to so many people to contribute to this book, and it shows up in our workshops, too.

Although David and I may be initiating and holding the group process, each participant makes his or her own contribution to the whole, and we love to see the ways in which people are able to support and facilitate eachother. The point of the workshop is that participants should leave with a deeper knowledge of themselves and their potential, and be able to offer something to others, if they so wish. We start out as a circle of students, sitting and listening solemnly to two teachers, and generally end up as a bunch of wise children, dancing together in shared freedom.

There is a saying in Zen, "When the realization is deep, your whole being is dancing." For realization to be complete, it has to hit on three levels — head, heart, and gut. You can have a very clear, enlightened mind, but your being won't be dancing. Then, when the heart starts to open along with the mind, your being starts to dance. Then everything comes alive. And when your gut opens up, there is that deep, deep, unfathomable stability where that opening, that is you, just died into transparency. You are dancing — the emptiness is dancing.[2]

chapter 27

The Gift of the Sufi

by Rahmana Dziubany

Rahmana has been on the Sufi path for twenty-five years. She is also an active dance leader and senior mentor for the Dances of Universal Peace. Please visit Rahmana.de or Dancesofuniversal-peace.org to learn more about the Sufi tradition and dances.

In one of the Islamic creation stories, we hear that the Creator wanted to realize Himself within creation. He offered to share His divine inheritance to manifest the light in this world. He was searching for a home, or as Ibn Arabi tells us, "I was a hidden treasure and wanted to be known; therefore I created the world." He called together the stones, the animals, the plants, and the first human beings, and asked them, *Alastubi Rabbikum*? In other words, "Do you agree that there is only one source of support and guidance behind all the diversity we see? Will you remember that there is only one reality that we all share, no matter what you call it?"

The first humans confirmed their readiness to witness and experience this phenomenon, consciously surrendering with full awareness that their bodies may be used to embody the divine light, to become an image of God on Earth. *La Ilaha Illallah: There is no reality but the One.*

This is the pure primordial light we find in the eyes of a newborn child. It is unveiled and unbroken, a little angel arriving on Earth. It reminds each of us of our original state, our oneness with God.

As we journey through our lives with all the tests and challenges we face, the veil of forgetfulness often covers our heart. We become disconnected from this blissful original state of being, feeling lost, empty, homeless, ignorant, and separate.

The human heart, to the Sufi, is a mirror catching this divine light and reflecting it out into the world. They know, as they walk through this life, that rust will collect on this mirror, and they recognize that their commitment to creation is to devotionally polish this mirror of the heart so that it can receive and radiate God's light.

The heart is the treasure chamber of God, say the Sufi, and holds the keys to open wide the doors of eternity. The heart is a garden, say the Sufi, which needs to be cultivated in order to blossom and bear rich fruit, bringing nourishment and healing to all. The Sufi mystics experienced this heart space as a garden of roses, filled with the scent of the Divine.

The gift of the Sufi is to return to us the memory of our true origins, the memory of all creation inherent in us, to open the hidden parts of our soul where we became separated from our divine potential. As we remember who we are, we become gardeners, digging deep in our hearts, sharing the rich harvest with all creation.

I first met Kiara twenty-eight years ago in Shantivanam, the ashram founded by Fr. Bede Griffiths in South India, as a gathering place for artists, writers, healers, scientists, backpackers, and pilgrims from all over the world. It was an experiment to bring together Eastern and Western spiritualities, science, and mysticism. By the holy river Cauvery, we danced and we sang in the remembrance of who we were.

In this location I also did the I Ch'ing oracle one day, which told me that I would lose all my belongings in order to find the destination of my soul. That very night, back home in Germany, my wooden hut in the forest burned down with all my worldly possessions. All the stories I had created in my life dissolved in the ashes, and I set my feet on this new path of becoming truly a lover of God. In India, they say that when the soul is ready to meet the teacher, the teacher will find you.

We each carry inside a longing for divine union. The Sufi call this the *Ishq* — the glue of the universe, which unites the longing ones. This Ishq gifted me with my Sufi teacher Pir Vilayat Inayat Khan, and years later brought me into the teaching of the Dances of Universal Peace — a deepening of my first encounter with the Sufi dances we shared on the banks of the holy Cauvery.

The dances are a joyful transformative tool to bring together people from all over the world, singing and dancing with prayers and mantras from different traditions. They were initially received by the first Sufi master of the West, Samuel L. Lewis, in the late 1960s. Sam was friend and teacher to the flower people and the hippies, and taught them that dances were a way to experience ecstasy without drugs, a way of saying yes to life, and of creating a strong sense of belonging to each other. Since his passing in 1972, the dances have spread worldwide, weaving a web of light through our dancing steps on the body of our Mother Gaia.

When Kiara and I left Father Bede's ashram, we lost touch with each other. Years went by until we finally met up again in the dance circles. Without knowing Kiara's background and story over the past decades, I received from him an Ilahinoor session. I felt a vibrant energy streaming through my body, taking me out into other dimensions, and then back into my body in a state of deep, deep relaxation.

As a senior mentor for the Dances of Universal Peace, I have trained hundreds of people to become dancers or dance teachers themselves. Using my feet as anchors for Mother Earth seemed so obvious and natural that it was a great shock to me to realize some years ago that my big toe had started to develop a serious form of arthritis, giving me pain and lack of balance, and making it difficult to even walk. The doctors told me there was nothing they could do for me, except to take cortisol to help with the pain and to prescribe special shoes. I tried various natural medicines and Chinese healing methods, which helped, but never really stopped the pain. Each step had become agony... but I kept dancing...

I had not heard of Ilahinoor before, so I had no expectations when he gave me a treatment. I do not really remember what and how it happened; I cannot recall if he put his hands on my body or if he touched my aura. I just remember this immense outpouring of light streaming through my body and transporting me into a world outside of time. I was in bliss, riding on a cosmic wave, not wanting to open my eyes or leave this magic space. I fell asleep and when I woke up in the morning I was still in such a blissful state that, when I took my first steps, I did not even realize that the pain was gone. I had forgotten that I had even suffered from this pain!

Now many months later... I am still without pain. I am dancing free-ly, taking my early morning jogs through the fields and forests of my home, and wearing my favorite red shoes again! I can still feel an arthritic condition in my toe, but the pain is completely gone, and my heart still feels that same blissful state as when Ilahinoor first started to stream through my body, heart, and soul.

I realized through experience that Ilahinoor sessions between two people can bring a very deep and rapid release of patterns, trau-mas, pain, or blockages within our bodies, hearts, and souls. As we make our inner journeys and then reconnect with the circle of life, we continue extending this web of light out to the world, so that what was found and released can now be embraced and cel-ebrated in a loving vibrant community with others.

When Ilahinoor and the Sufi dances can be shared together, I have experienced a deep power of healing. Where the dances bring healing through sound, movement, and breath as a group, the Ilahinoor work allows the sound of the universe to resonate within all the cells of our body, freeing the soul and releasing what has been stuck.

I am writing this now as I visit a Sufi sister in the aboriginal lands of Australia. She has been challenged by a life-threatening illness for some months. While we dance in her dance temple, I work on her with the gift of Ilahinoor. We both feel this light protection and the calmness and peace it brings, allowing her to find inner rest, contacting her deepest inner hidden self and finally helping her to find some sleep. Her spirit is so bright and shining that we tend to overlook that her body is in pain.

All over the world, we pray for this precious one and send Ilahinoor; we cannot tell how her story will unfold. In this painful struggle with the limitations of her body, the Ilahinoor work, as well as the songs of life, bring ease, comfort, protection, and joy. My dear friend tells me: When I arrive at the beach of stars, I will not have left you. We only share this one reality, and we promised the Creator that we would witness and experience this. *La Ilaha il Allah*.

The message of my Sufi lineage is one of spiritual freedom and liberation. "Dare to be *the one* you really are," or as we sing it in one of our songs, *Return again, return again, return to the land of your soul. Return to who you are, return to what you are, return to where you are born and reborn again.*

Ilahinoor and the Dances of Universal Peace, together with other Sufi practices of breath, sound, and movement, are ready to guide us along this path as eternal friends and companions. Thus, we enter the garden of our hearts, each with our own unique story of unfoldment and healing, and yet united in the heart of the One. Ilahinoor is a beautiful gateway into this garden. Through the dances, connecting heart to heart in one circle, singing as one voice and as one body, we can receive even deeper this divine light. Both the dances and Ilahinoor are a means of polishing our hearts and becoming vessels of this divine light.

I am grateful for the reunion with my dear friend Kiara Windrider, who has devoted his life to being a vessel and channel for this healing stream, helping his fellow human beings become vessels and channels themselves. His work, his being, and his radical surrender to the divine call is of great significance for the evolutionary process of Mother Earth. I am touched, I feel healed, and I am following this call as well, making Ilahinoor a vibrant breathing reality at my International Institute for Dance and Peace Arts near Berlin. May you all feel the gift of Ilahinoor and the blessing of our dancing steps, which weave patterns of heavenly light into the body of our beloved Earth Mother.

chapter 28

Techniques for Transmission

by Arthur Collins

Arthur is a spiritual activist who has been involved with creating bridges between indigenous traditions and the major world religions, particularly Tibetan Buddhism. His website is WorldOnenessCenter.com.

———◇———

We are so blessed to be alive during these amazing times. We are a transitional group of beings helping humanity move from one way of being to another. We have often been called the *transitional generation*, the last generation of the old, and the first generation of the new.

Wow! This is a big gift, and a big responsibility. We are the change our ancestors have described, we are the ones tearing down the walls of separation, and opening the channels of unity and compassion for all.

Our stories are unique, yet overlapping. How quickly life is unfolding, and how much grace is being poured into us and through us! Our bodies and psyches often shake and vibrate for no reason; tears well up as our hearts expand in a longing to reach out and heal those struggling or in need. We realize this experience is all part of our journey toward universal wholeness and a sense of global family.

As we move closer to a time of Shift, humanity is beginning to choose love and compassion over war and hate, acceptance and understanding over condemnation and denial. The scenarios of a world destroying itself are being replaced with new directions of healing and mending hearts. Rather than judging ourselves for what we have been, a deep compassion is unfolding. We are our ancestors and our descendents alike, we are the hurts, the fears, and the shame alike. And now we are moving into deeper and deeper levels of understanding and love for all beings, all humanity.

Ilahinoor has come to us as a beautiful gift of love that helps us to embody our chosen path of divine embodiment. Many have shared so many beautiful rich and inspiring insights into the nature of Ilahinoor and how it is touching lives and assisting in the shift of human consciousness. The collective mind of man and the grace of the divine are working hand in hand to assist this process.

As we get closer to a time of planetary ascension, we are being invited to release the fears, distortions, and patterns that keep us separate. Ilahinoor, for me, aligns all aspects of the self, from our deepest shadows to our *I AM Presence*.

I started offering Ilahinoor workshops combining Ilahinoor with Tibetan Healing techniques I had learned while living among Tibetans in Dharmsala and Bodhgaya, India. This effort was essentially about connecting with the field of Ilahinoor first at the level of the receiver's *I AM Presence*, then gradually bringing it down to their *Soul Star* a couple feet above their head, then down into the *Crown*, down the *Central Channel*, and then down through their *Earth Star* deep into the core of Mother Earth. As this connection occurred, the individual's aura would realign itself and correct various issues from the past.

I saw that when people experienced some kind of traumatic event, they would be attuned to certain vibrations of fear or discord. These vibrations would be held within the person's aura, then flow down through their aura into the crown chakra and the rest of the energy system. To my amazement, attuning with Ilahinoor corrected all of that, disconnecting the earlier traumas and realigning everything through the individual's *I AM*. Folks were moved and tears flowed and flowed.

Release of the Underworlds

One process that has recently taken form for me is healing the collective and personal in all realms, including the underworlds. I cannot convey strongly enough the importance of this work.

I have recently been guided to start work in the *hell realms*, and some amazing things are occurring. I am being shown many different aspects of this realm — how and why they were created, and their roles in the evolution of humanity.

Many beings — perhaps even aspects of ourselves from the past — have been were told that what they were doing is wrong and for it they were condemned to *hell*. What I was clearly shown was that this belief in condemnation was lodged deep in the subconscious fields of humanity, but that it is easy now to *un*condemn ourselves.

While in Bodhgaya, close to the banyan tree where the Buddha received his enlightenment, a friend and I shamanically went into the depths of hell and planted a Tree of Life. Many of us have such a strong belief in condemnation and hell that these beliefs create their own reality on some level, contributing also to the creation of a hell on Earth. We can reverse this phenomenon by creating love and light in the hell realms, which we did by anchoring the unified light of Ilahinoor in the image of a Tree of Life.

So many beautiful gifts and aspects of life have been wrongly condemned as well, and have been locked up in the subconscious hell realms of our mind. It is time to uncondemn them, and to release them back to humanity and to nature.

As the Earth undergoes a Shift, our cocreated hells must also shift in structure. I was shown how so many beings took the roles of *devils* and *demons* for our evolution. Now they can start to complete their roles and return to the place beyond good and evil, right and wrong, light and dark. Ilahinoor is a beautiful light guiding their path home.

We can help by simply anchoring this light into the leylines and meridian points of the Earth, and also by embracing our own shadows. As this experience happens, the light radiates through the collective fields of humanity and the Earth, and those who believe they deserved hell can be healed and set free. This effort is all part of creating heaven on Earth.

What I see happening for Mother Earth is so wonderful. Her leylines and timelines are being cleared of mental overlays by aspects of humanity still locked in the illusion of control. It's so wonderful, we are all — and I do mean *all* — part of a remarkable shift taking place; I am so grateful for Ilahinoor and for the help I have received in guiding me in my own personal role within this collective shift.

The Oneness Healing Meditation

The Oneness Healing Meditation (OHM) is a highly effective procedure for using the Divine Grace and Angelic Assistance in a number of areas of life. It can be very helpful in assisting us in various aspects of daily life, as well as in our ascension process. It can be used on a daily basis, and used anytime you are feeling down or lacking in energy and vitality. It is a great procedure to undertake when you wish to turn your dreams into reality. And it can be shared with others either directly or over the phone.

Before starting the OHM, let us review briefly some aspects of brain science that may explain how Divine Grace in the form of Ilahinoor works to cleanse our lives of stress and brings us increasing states of joy and fulfillment.

The brain produces certain chemicals known as neuro-peptides.

There are neuro-peptides associated with every emotional state that we experience, such as fear, love, anger, depression, and so forth. As they flow through our nervous systems, these neuro-peptides are attracted to cells that have receptor sites linked to various emotional states. They fit into these receptors just like a key fits into a lock.

If a certain emotion is predominant in a person, the production of peptides related to that emotion tends to increase. When cell division occurs, the receptors of the daughter cell will be structured to receive the peptide related to that emotion. If these receptors are matched with lower vibrational emotions such as depression, fear, and hatred, the cells are not able to receive nutrients or to release toxins. This phenomenon accelerates the aging process and results in physical and mental sickness.

A small input of energy has the power to bring order to a system that is full of chaos. Ilahinoor may be used to assist in the transfer of divine energy that brings order into the brain, resulting in healing and balancing the mind and body. It ultimately activates dormant aspects within the DNA, which allow neuro-peptides related to higher emotions such as love, joy, and fulfillment to predominate.

While performing this meditation, intend for the Ilahinoor Energy and Divine Grace to cleanse and purify your cells, receive whatever nutrients are needed, and create structures that are in harmony with a happy and fulfilled life style.

The Oneness Healing Meditation described here may be used to receive blessings in all areas of your life. It may also be used by groups to bring healing and blessings to one's group, family, community, and the planet.

Blessings may be invoked for physical healing, emotional healing, or for manifesting abundance, harmony, and peace in the world.

Take a moment to decide what you would like to pray for and then begin your session from a place of gratitude.

During the OHM, you will be sitting down and moving your legs and arms into some very simple yet highly beneficial postures. These postures are based on the work of Dr. Fred Gallo and Donna Eden in the field of Energy Medicine and Energy Psychology.

For the Oneness Healing Meditation you will need to be seated in order to properly perform the following steps.

1. Start by holding an intention in mind. For example, your intention could be to deepen your experience of oneness, or to bring healing into a relationship, or to create financial freedom in your life. It could be to release a specific fear or addiction in your life, or to achieve peace and harmony in the world.

2. Take a moment to align with your intention and call in your Guardian Angel. Ask your personal Angel, who has been with you since your creation, to assist you here today. Offer your intentions and gratitude to the Divine, and simply sit in the Presence for a few moments.

3. Cross your left ankle over your right. Hold your hands out in front of you, arms extended, with your palms facing one another. Next, turn your hands over so that your thumbs point down and the back of your hands are now touching each other. Raise your right hand up and over your left hand, and interlock the fingers. Now turn your hands in and up so that your hands are resting on your chest under your chin.

4. Now place the tip of your tongue at the roof of your mouth behind the little ridge at the center of the palate. Take some slow, deep diaphragmatic breaths in through your nose. At this point, it is helpful to gently close your eyes and breathe slowly and deeply. Imagine that the breath is coming in through the bottom of your

feet all the way up through your body. Comfortably hold in mind your intention and prayer request as you breathe.

5. While breathing this way, visualize the Ilahinoor and Divine Grace shining down from the heavens and onto your head. Imagine that this light comes in through the top of your head as you breathe in and then travels throughout your body, vibrating into every cell, every fiber of your being, from the top of your head all the way down into your shoulders and back, chest and stomach, legs and arms, feet and hands. Continue this experience for a little while, and comfortably bring your intention and prayer request into your awareness as you continue to breathe.

6. Now unlock your fingers, arms, and legs and set your feet flat on the floor, placing your hands and fingers in a prayer-like position, the fingertips of the left hand touching the fingertips of the right hand. While you hold this position, continue to position the tip of your tongue to the roof of your mouth and breathe slowly and steadily. Continue to sense Ilahinoor light glowing throughout your body. As you inhale, imagine and feel the breath coming up through the bottom of your feet. Maintain this position for a minute or two. Comfortably remain aware of your intention in doing this process.

7. Now relax for a moment or two and notice how you feel. Gently relax and allow your hands and arms to rest gently on your thighs. Take a few breaths, simply relaxing and noticing any sensations you may be experiencing. Just be with your breath and remain calm for a few moments.

8. Next, place the index and middle finger of one hand on your forehead between your eyebrows, just lightly touching. Take in a deep breath from your diaphragm and slowly exhale. Affirm three times each of the following statements:

- I am eliminating any remaining aspects of this problem from my whole being — mind, body, and soul. I am releasing all toxins from my entire body and all my cells.

- I am creating balance and harmony throughout my entire being, activating the frontal lobes of the brain and deactivating the parietal lobes.

- Divine Grace is fulfilling my intentions comfortably and easily bringing grace and harmony into all areas of my life.

9. Next, place the two fingers under your nose, breathe slowly, and make the same affirmation three times each.

10. Next, place the two fingers under your bottom lip, breathe slowly, and make the same affirmation three times each.

11. Next, place the fingertips on your upper chest, and continue breathing. Tap lightly on your chest as you make the same affirmation three times each.

12. Next, place the palm of one hand over the center of your chest. Get in touch with your feelings of love, compassion, beauty, and joy, and ask for the Divine Blessing to flow into you. Notice the color of this energy flow. Feel the Divine Grace of Ilahinoor entering your heart, and send this healing love to your entire being. Give thanks to the Divine for all the wonderful love and light you continue to receive.

13. Taking your time, return your awareness to your surroundings, and allow yourself time to reorient. Reconsider your intentions for this process. In most instances, the symptoms will be relieved or entirely gone. If your intentions were for joy and deeper experiences of oneness, you will most likely feel a much richer and fuller experience of this emotion throughout your entire being.

Most people will feel a deep sense of peace, calmness, and love, even when this experience was not a part of their stated intentions.

You may repeat this process as often as you'd like. I wish you much joy and happiness as you move into full awakening and oneness with the cosmos.

The Forgiveness Meditation/Prayer

Forgiveness helps to open the door to freedom, harmony, and peace by rewriting the scripts of the past. We are all expressions of a unique soul journey that crosses many dimensions and time-lines. As such, we can we rewrite scripts related to trauma, war, old debts, and karmic obligation.

These old energies greatly influence our collective future by keeping old wounds alive. Through forgiveness, we bring light into the dark and heal the past, thus changing our experience of the future. Instead of continuing to replay old scripts, we can welcome new energies, bathing our planet in love, harmony, and truth.

Nothing unreal can last, and nothing real can ever be destroyed. As lightworkers, our thoughts, feelings, and attitudes contribute mightily to anchoring a new light on Earth. Like a lighthouse shining its light so that sailors can find safe passage through the storms, so, too, can we keep shining our light for others to find their way home — whether we are aware of this service or not.

Forgiveness helps us take the shutters off the lighthouses within, allowing this light to shine a little brighter, releasing wounds from the past, cancelling old debts, and eradicating karmic patterns. Instead of oppressing and fighting each other based on events or teachings from the past, we can start anew in present time, choosing what worlds we wish to create from a place of love, integrity, and dignity.

Call on the Ilahinoor field and offer forgiveness to yourself and others for whatever wrongs — real or imagined — we may have done to others, or may have been done unto us from others. I have devised the following prayer to start things off:

On behalf of my soul's journey through all time and space
on all levels and dimensions... both seen and unseen...
known and unknown
If I have caused any hurt or pain, be it real or imagined,
purposeful or accidental, I apologize and seek forgiveness.
And, if anyone else on their soul's journey
through all time and space
on all levels and dimensions... both seen and unseen...
known and unknown
has caused any hurt or pain, be it real or imagined,
purposeful or accidental,
All is forgiven and all is released.
At the Soul level, all contracts are complete,
all debts have been paid
and all Karma is balanced.
As we accept and embrace the Joy and Enlightenment
that is unfolding upon the planet at this time,
We ask the Divine Presence to bring Divine Grace
into this area of our lives...
Ilahinoor Ilahinoor Ilahinoor

chapter 29

A Grandmaster's Story

by Peter Herriger

Peter is a grandmaster in the Pit Kune Do tradition, and maintains an academy for teaching self-defense and close-quarter combat systems. He has also been working extensively in the field of energy medicine. Peter and his wife, Sophia, live in Ludwigsburg, Germany, and can be reached through Ilahinoor4you.com and P-k-d.info.

———○———

I first met Kiara about five years ago at one of his lectures in Stuttgart, Germany. He spoke about the evolution of Earth and humanity with a simplicity and conviction that touched me. As he spoke about Ilahinoor, I felt an energy in the room that rippled through my whole organism and subtle bodies. My perceptions felt more expanded, and I could feel my energy centers responding to an inner light, which convinced me that something profound was happening.

For over thirty-five years, I have been involved in martial arts as well as different healing systems and meditation practices. I have been studying psychology and esoteric wisdom for many years. I hold the titles of Grandmaster and Professor in martial arts and psycho-physiology. I have studied shamanism and trained my body to survive in wilderness situations. I have studied nutrition and preventive health systems. All this has served my health, cultivated my life energy, and helped me to advise others.

Kiara's methods for expanding consciousness, his ability to convey this message, and his energy frequency resonated with me. I liked his philosophy of sharing Ilahinoor generously so that many humans could enjoy its healing benefits and participate in the collective awakening of consciousness. I liked the idea of having a tool, a spiritual vehicle, that enabled us to connect with cosmic energy fields for the greatest possible benefits — so that we could transform our nature from human to divine.

My partner, Sophia, and I decided to attend his weekend seminar. We learned to practice Ilahinoor with each other, along with shamanic breath work and Sufi dancing. We experienced a loving, feminine, gentle energy that permeated all our cell structures as well as the subtle bodies. It created feelings of oneness and being connected with everything. This feeling accompanied each participant and endured even after the seminar ended.

Sophia and I continued practicing the Ilahinoor techniques after this weekend. Kiara had told us these tools were useful for self-healing, and for cleansing the body and mind of addictions and negativity. He was right. They were easy to apply, and a few minutes of daily practice gave us wonderful experiences of this powerful energetic work.

Later, I attended a five-day retreat with Kiara. I had no special expectations, but was curious about what I would experience. Most of the participants at the retreat were also healing arts professionals. Kiara's teachings and the treatments we practiced on each other worked very deeply on mental, emotional, and physiological layers. I had uncountable visions of past life experiences and encounters with my shamanic guides. From time to time, I felt like my body was cooking from the intensity of the energies passing through it. Various parapsychological phenomena were happening, but without painful physical symptoms. I found I could watch the whole process with a kind of humorous detachment as my body went through all kinds of spectacular reactions.

A quintessential moment of awakening occurred when I realized that the individual self does not exist. This cosmic joke, an indescribable, incomprehensible paradoxical self-realization had revealed itself to me. I was pure awareness, a universal consciousness that could not be identified with any physical reality in time and space. I can confirm that illumination indeed happens in one instant of recognition. The conception of the old self had died and a new perception of reality was introduced into my consciousness.

I understood that maintaining and cultivating the awareness of this creative consciousness, which was accompanied by an inner peace and silence, would require life-long, loving care. Something pure and natural that had always deeply been a part of me had been reborn. We all carry IT in us from birth. To recognize this truth was for me an experience that burst all the conceptions I had known in philosophical writings of world religions and philosophies, because the process of awakening has nothing to do with our intellect. It is a pure biological, human process of development soaked in divine grace, light, and love.

The following remarkable episode describes a further experience of the Ilahinoor field, which took place after several years of integration. I was taking my usual after-lunch nap with my cat, Lucas, when suddenly and unexpectedly I found myself in Egypt, amongst the pyramids, immersed in Ilahinoor rays of light.

I was lying on the couch with my eyes closed and hands resting on the belly to help my digestion when Lucas came and settled down on my chest. I was dozing along, not really thinking about anything in particular. Suddenly, a vision appeared before my third eye. I was standing between three enormous pyramids. Above me was a point where the energies of the pyramids were focused together. The Sun was just above the horizon to the left of me. I heard an enormous roar above me. As I looked up, three rays of light were coming from the pyramids around me, meeting together and splitting into two directions, one downward and one upward. Out of this bastion of light, a bright current flowed into my chest and filled my body. Simultaneously, a flash of lightening penetrated my chest, expanding my heart chakra, and spreading to the rest of my body.

At that very second, my tomcat jumped as quick as a flash from my chest and leaped off to the side. All his hair was standing on end, which made him appear oversized. Astonished, we looked at each other. His questioning eyes stared at me from a safe distance.

Then, I closed my eyes again, wishing to go back to the scene of the pyramids; however, the visual experience among the pyramids was over. Only the immense energy of these light rays, brighter and more radiant than any sunbeam, was still clearly perceivable. It filled my entire body and beyond. I felt waves and waves of expansion and needed a good thirty minutes to calm down. Breathing deeply helped my nervous system adapt to these subtle light frequencies.

I needed a few days to digest this intensive adventure. I am infinitely grateful for this spiritual highlight! It was, for me, convincing living proof that an age-old, preserved consciousness and light field, which is active on the Giza plateau in Egypt, exists. It also confirmed that I, personally, have a connection to the world-wide pyramid culture and its energy field, which I had fostered for years. The vision leading up to the energy transfer took some minutes. The light contact afterward was short, but enormous amounts of information, bundled in rays of light, flowed in through my body and spirit, where they are stored.

I have so far had extremely positive experiences with the Ilahinoor field. The more this energy flows, the more it uncovers light codes within the cells, allowing a deeper rejuvenation to take place. Friends who have known me for decades are surprised at how little I seem to have aged. When the physical body connects with the light body, a divine ascent starts to happen. I feel young, happy, dynamic, and joyful. Inside I feel calm, centered, and balanced — tranquility in motion!

I guess we could call this youth research. Interestingly, because of this light experience, my former urge to follow the mystic call and plan a longer journey to Egypt isn't as strong anymore. This experience was most certainly a key moment in my spiritual journey.

I find that whether I am treating myself, someone else, or giving Ilahinoor over a distance, Ilahinoor flows through my organism, reaches the recipient and goes to where it is most needed. If no special intention is expressed before beginning, the physical intelligence directs the energy flow. As I review the last five years during which I have been working with the Ilahinoor field, I realize that several abilities and latent talents have come to light and further developed.

After practicing Ilahinoor regularly for a while, this light frequency has become second nature and appears whenever it is needed. Once we have activated ourselves as a channel — letting the energy flow through us — an internal light fills our heart and physical being. Each time we connect with the field, even just thinking of Ilahinoor, it enhances our ability to trust in divine guidance. I am learning to think with my heart and feel with my intellect. Harmony, peace, love, understanding, intuition, introspection, and mindfulness have become steady companions on my journey.

There is not an area of our lives where we do not feel protected by the Ilahinoor field. Here are a few examples:

We live in an area of Germany that is often very stormy. Between the years 2000 and 2005, the neighbourhood we moved into was regularly flooded and basements had to be pumped dry. After moving to our block in 2006, my wife and I applied a ritual that we call the *Ilahinoor Pyramid*. Since then not just our house but also those of the neighbours have been protected from flooding, even though we often read in the morning's local newspaper that damage was done by storms in the vicinity.

Many times while driving long distances, I have also felt the protection and guidance of Ilahinoor. My attention span is much greater and my intuition keener. I always arrive at my destination with ease, and without uncomfortable incidents, even if things do not go according to plan. A pattern of Ilahinoor intervention has often revealed itself. When driving, I have sudden impulses to react in a way I had not planned. This response often happens when potential danger, traffic jams, or other obstacles are ahead.

Using Ilahinoor in our healing practice has been very beneficial. We work with a variety of holistic healing methods, combining Ilahinoor, meditation, movement, and manual therapies. By using Ilahinoor in this way, we have obtained better results with our treatments. Many people find relief from physical pain, motor disorders, joint problems, paralysis, and posture problems. The Ilahinoor treatment of the spine is especially effective.

Of course our nutrition plays an extremely important role in health prevention. Before eating, we energize and bless all food with Ilahinoor divine energy and grace. We let the light energy simply flow from our palms, transferring it to our food. In addition, one can speak a prayer, sing a song, make a positive affirmation, or express an intention for a specific healing purpose.

My wife and I have five cats. They all love and enjoy receiving Ilahinoor transmissions from us. One day, our cat Lucas experienced kidney failure, which is common for cats his age. The vet had given him a few hours to live. For three days, we gave him an infusion with vitamins and minerals, because he refused to eat and had lost so much weight, while treating him several times a day with Ilahinoor. He recovered, and would afterward come for an Ilahinoor session on his own whenever he felt the need for it. Animals also respond well to remote treatments with Ilahinoor.

Ilahinoor treatments on the joints and the spinal column help my Kung Fu students develop greater flexibility and coordination. I personally use these treatments as I lie in bed each morning, energetically and physically connecting the joints and skeletal system. Morning stiffness disappears, and injuries heal quickly.

I include Ilahinoor when I teach Kung Fu to children. They are very enthusiastic and easily feel the energy. Parents confirm that their children are always more balanced on the days we practice Ilahinoor, and it seems to help them in the rest of their schoolwork as well. These are the only lessons during which the children are totally concentrated. The whale music that I use to accompany these lessons seems to have a calming effect on them as well.

Sophie and I feel so guided and blessed by Ilahinoor. We feel a deep gratitude for this divine blessing, and are honoured to serve Earth, humanity, and our collective awakening in this way. We thank Kiara for his untiring enthusiasm and love, and for allowing himself to be a doorway in this evolutionary process.

chapter 30

Enlightenment and Burnout

by Sophia Hildebrand

Sophia lives with her husband, Peter, and daughter, Alexandra, near Ludwigsburg, Germany, and can be reached at p-k-d@t-online.de

———○———

Let me shortly describe my own spiritual development before I came to know Kiara and Ilahinoor. As a child, I had the ability, as many children do, to discern spirits, and had a natural talent for being clairvoyant. My parents were quite distressed when I talked about my experiences and dismissed them as nonsense. So I kept everything to myself.

For many years, I suppressed these abilities, until I traveled with a friend to Italy, where I had two special experiences. The first experience took place during a tour of Pompeii. Suddenly, I found myself, as if in a film, in the city as it was 2,000 years before. Not only was I in this ancient city, but I could also see the people who lived there at that time. When I got home, I did some research and was able to verify that what I had seen was accurate. The second experience was on the island of Capri, where again, in the middle of the day, I experienced myself as a priestess who was thrown off a cliff. Afterward, I could not walk for two hours.

These experiences motivated me to rediscover my long-forgotten abilities. My interest in shamanism grew. I had always felt a strong connection to indigenous people. I also knew that there was more between heaven and Earth than meets the eye. When my husband, Peter, came into my life twenty years ago, we began a new spiritual journey together. We lived almost two years in northern Greece where we established Kung Fu schools. We trained in *cluster medicine*, which is a complementary holistic diagnosis and therapy method. We read a lot of spiritual and esoteric literature, experimented with out-of-body experiences, and visited many shamans and teachers. We were particularly interested in the advaita teachings focused on enlightenment and nonduality.

I met Kiara in 2006, and since then have taken many seminars with him. Each experience was different; they have opened up a profound path of discovery and healing for me, including healing from alcoholism. I am delighted to say that I have not touched alcohol nor even felt the need for it for over four years now.

Since I started working with Ilahinoor I have became closely connected with the whales and the dolphins. They live in my heart, communicate with me, answer my questions, share with me how they are feeling, and tell me about the changes that will take place on Earth.

What happens with us when we become a channel for Ilahinoor energy? First and foremost, this experience opens our hearts. It connects our bodies with our spirit and souls. The more often we work with the energy, the more we are connected with the Ilahinoor field. For me it is enough just to think about Ilahinoor and the energy is there. I AM the energy! It brings forth latent abilities and strengthens individual gifts. After working with Ilahinoor for five years now, Ilahinoor has blessed me in many ways. Some of them are listed below.

- An ancient knowledge of healing and shamanic skills has manifested.
- My natural talent for clairvoyance has developed.
- When healing with my hands, I can visualize where the energy is blocked in the body and understand which level of the soul is involved.

- I find myself able to merge simply with nature, water, trees, leaves, clouds.
- I have taken wonderful journeys to other dimensions.
- When totally connected with the Ilahinoor field, I receive messages from shamans or spirit beings about future events. I can communicate with them and my questions are answered. I combine Ilahinoor with different kinds of methods of healing, but also in the activities of daily life. It has helped me become aware of my shadows, and also to release them. I am neither afraid to go into these shadow places anymore nor to go into the depths of my soul.

Being a channel for Ilahinoor makes it easier to access other energy fields as well — as I discovered at one of Kiara's seminars in Switzerland. One day, a massive ray of white light entered into me through the crown chakra and passed through my spinal column. I identified this light as an energy field from Sirius. Since then I have been working with both of these light fields, and one or both of these energies might come through in a healing session, depending on what is needed.

One day, I had the following extraordinary experience of awakening. I was on my way to a lovely spot in nature where I go to replenish my energy. I was feeling totally one with Mother Earth and the cosmos. I connected myself with the energy field of Ilahinoor and Sirius. I asked them to show me what enlightenment is. I got the answer already on the way back to the car. I didn't expect it so soon! While I was walking, a window opened in my mind and everything was quiet all of a sudden.

There was no thought, no identification with a *me*, no fear, no emotions, no evaluations, just pure awareness and absolute stillness. I have no idea how long this experience lasted because I had no feeling for time or space. Then I understood that thought, identification, fears, evaluations, and so forth existed only in the duality. I felt bliss; I was absolutely free, blessed with an all-comprehensive love. The tears ran down my cheeks with joy. I laughed and danced!

I just could not believe how simple everything was! How can I find the right words to describe this experience? It is glorious to feel so connected with everything. It changed me and the quality of my life. When I got to my car (I can't remember how I got there), I could not move. I was in a completely different mode of being. After a while, I could move again and drove home. Well, actually the car was driven home with me in it. That is how it felt! Once at home, I ran around constantly crying out, "I can't believe this, everything is so simple!" I knew intuitively, without needing a confirmation by someone else, that this event was an experience of awakening. For ten weeks, I remained in this wonderful state. I recognized also that awakening means being constantly aware of myself and that it would take a steady effort to integrate and cultivate this consciousness.

Two weeks after this experience, my daughter became seriously ill. She experienced a total collapse of body, mind, and soul, accompanied by nausea, dizziness, cramping, and trouble breathing. She was eventually diagnosed with a bad case of *burnout syndrome*. My awakening has been an incredible source of support, helping me and my daughter deal with this situation.

For two months, she was bed-ridden with violent pains in her spine, bones, inner organs, muscles, and skin. She was treated medically, given pharmaceutical medicines and infusions, but nothing helped. Her complaints even worsened. At some point, she was diagnosed with burnout, which led her to psychologists and behavioral therapists. Further prescriptions of allopathic drugs just aggravated her condition. She stopped all medications.

During these weeks, the only thing that helped her was when I gave her energy transmissions. I have no idea how often we worked in this way. Whenever she had a depressive episode, day or night, we worked with the light fields of Ilahinoor and Sirius. It was the only thing that could relieve her pain and relax her enough so that she could fall asleep. Every time she was overcome by panic or pain, I would first softly stroke the physical and subtle bodies, which cooled down areas of the body that were overheated.

Afterwards, I would do an energy transmission, letting light and love flow down through the crown chakra, along with some grounding exercises. Massage helped, and I found I could also stimulate the internal organs with light energy. I developed a new way of working with the spine using subtle vibrations, which was also very useful. Sometimes mental and physical blockages dissolved immediately; other times, the healing took place slowly and quietly. Sometimes a complaint would intensify and then suddenly dissolve. We could tell the energy treatments were helping because we recognized a positive change in her attitude and behavior. In some parts of her body, the pain fully disappeared.

During the last two months, we have seen definite improvement in our daughter's health. The fear comes less often and less intensively. Her psychosomatic complaints are much better as well. After searching for months, we have also found a health center that treats burnout with holistic healing methods. We are very confident that the roughest part of her journey is over and that Alexandra will soon be healthy enough to master her life again independently. She has developed a deep sense of her own spirituality during these long and difficult weeks, and it has been very impressive to see how clearly her latent psychic abilities are beginning to manifest.

We are all connected to each other. Our hopes, desires, thoughts, feelings, and knowledge all flow into one cosmic river that holds us all. Everything is a dream that can be changed and be transformed at any moment. We can bring light and love into this great cosmic river, to share and pass on to others. May each of you be embraced and blessed by the divine grace of these cosmic energy fields!

chapter 31

My Discovery of Ilahinoor

by Sean Copping-Rice

Sean is a healer and channel living in Cape Town, South Africa. He has created a facebook group, LoveOneness, and can be reached at ilahinoorlight@gmail.com.

———◇———

Ilahinoor, Divine Light. This amazing and peaceful energy came to me by the grace of the divine over a series of experiences. Having opened myself to the Deeksha phenomenon, which acted as the first doorway, my consciousness shifted just enough for the Guides and Angels to introduce me to this powerful Light.

The Light first came to me in a meditation at my home, where I found myself standing up, eyes open, in awe of a most beautiful vortex of golden light that had manifested before me. It looked like sparks swirling in an ever-growing spiral of cosmic fire. I thought it was the Deeksha energy at the time.

It happened to me again in my meditation circle. We did a meditation with Lord Ashtar and Mother Earth, in which we were invoking Divine Light into the Earth, and I saw the Earth turn into a massive golden orb of fire that had the same golden sparks emanating from it. I felt the Light move instantly into my heart; again, we thought it was Deeksha, as it was our intention at the time.

Later, after our Circles instructor, Maia, went to India to attend the then twenty-one-day Deeksha process, she was approached by Ashtar again to bring this energy to the Circle. We did a three-month process, receiving Deeksha each week and working with the teachings we were given. We stopped eating meat so as to raise our vibrations. One day, Archangel Michael stood before me during a Deeksha blessing session and told me to stand up and give the blessing. Other Deeksha givers were there from outside our circle that day and they knew I was not a Deeksha giver.

I said to Michael, "No, I can't, what will the Deeksha givers think if I just stand up and start giving Deeksha, I haven't been to India to do the process." Michael said firmly, "Stand Up! It's only your fear that is holding you back." At that point, my hands started to burn as if on fire and it was incredibly uncomfortable. I knew that in order to stop it, I had to stand.

So I did. I stood up and placed my hands on the person next to me. A rush moved through me. I moved from one person to the next, and the energy seemed to get stronger and stronger. At the end, one of the Deeksha givers asked what had happened and why I had stood up. So I explained to her what Michael had said. One of the persons receiving the energy said that she saw a golden man standing before her and that the energy she had felt was amazing.

Shortly afterward, we went on a three-day retreat to ground the energy, as Ashtar had instructed. Our Circles instructor, Maia, decided not to give any Deeksha that weekend so as not to interfere with the energy we were giving. I started sharing the blessing, and others there started getting up spontaneously and sharing the energy.

It was one of the most amazing experiences I think I've ever had. I completely transformed into the Archangel Gabriel the whole time I was there. Archangel Michael, Ashtar, and other guides were also with us through the process. The energy was so strong that pure white feathers manifested all over the room during the next three days.

One experience in particular was when Gabriel gave the blessing through me. I felt my center of gravity shift as I became completely female. I could see her toes, feel her pure white flowing dress, feel her wings. It was as though my own body did not exist and I was experiencing myself as Gabriel. As the Blessing was given, Gabriel folded her wings around the lady that was receiving, and then suddenly flung them open wide and a massive light shone out. The lady receiving the energy started to shake as her *Kundalini* activated. At the end of the session, as we were leaving the room, I noticed that a perfect pure white feather stuck to her dress close to her shoulder. I don't believe in coincidences, so I believe this feather was a manifestation of that experience.

Upon returning to our normal weekly circle, we started some channelings to see if this experience was really the Deeksha energy with which we had connected. In these channelings, we were told that it was not Deeksha but a new energy and, at the same time, a very old energy originating in Africa. We were confused. We asked what it was called but the Guides simply said, "Do not put this energy into a box, it is simply grace, it has no name." We insisted that for practical purposes we get a name for the energy, so the Guides said to call it Divine Grace and left it at that.

The very next day, as I sat on my computer, I mistyped a word in the google search engine and Kiara's website *Ilahinoor.net* came up. The word compelled me to it. I started reading the website and as I saw the word *Ilahinoor* I heard the voice of Archangel Gabriel say, "This is what you can call it, this is what it is!" I felt waves of excitement move through me and a sudden deep connection and resonance.

Ever since then, the energy has deepened in me. I have since also become a Deeksha giver and a Sai Maa Diksha Trainer, but this vibration holds a special place in my heart. I feel that my recent attraction to Sai Maa Diksha is because the form of Diksha that Sai Maa has blessed to the world is somehow linked to Ilahinoor. I feel Ilahinoor in the Diksha, almost as though knowingly or unknowingly Sai Maa has merged this grace with the form of grace of her own lineage to bring a powerful transmission to us at this time. Archangel Gabriel had told me that Ilahinoor is birthed from the womb of the Divine Mother. Maa is also a manifestation of the Divine Mother. Is this why I feel the link?

Ultimately all forms of Divine Light are the same. But I do experience subtle differences. The vast tranquility and soft soothing motherly love of Ilahinoor is by far my favorite experience of Divine Light and the one closest to my heart.

I would like to share next a transmission from Archangel Gabriel on Ilahinoor:

Greetings Beloveds, I Am the Archangel Gabriel.

Ilahinoor, Ilahinoor, Ilahinoor, this amazing word acts as a gateway to the vibration that is Ilahinoor. This supreme grace is the vibration that is here at this time to bring great changes into the world and to the universe. We, the Archangels, Angels, Ascended Masters, and Cosmic Beings are blessed to be the Guides for this divine gift in the world, and all who openly wish to connect with this energy will receive its blessings.

It is our hope to generate a momentum for this process so that the race of humanity can shift from human to divine. Ilahinoor is that tool given to humanity in order to ensure that this shift takes place. Beloved ones, you are the vehicles that will transform your world and the universe to the next level of existence. As your Guides, we speak to you now from a higher point of view to guide you into a place where you will no longer need us. We are integrating with you on every level now. We are One.

The grace of Ilahinoor is the power of Oneness manifesting within you. It works in your consciousness as well as within your bodies, starting with the brain and heart centers. You see, the universal mind is One with the universal heart and it is the same in you. You will come to realize this; the field of ilahinoor will awaken this understanding within you. You already know this on a cellular level but Ilahinoor will awaken this cellualr memory in a graceful, loving way that is not something that needs to happen, but rather something that is to be remembered. Ilahinoor will give you remembrance in a graceful loving way that is not a huge shock to you.

At that point, your DNA will begin to mutate, transforming your body into a pure undense light. This experience is called ascension, which many believe will occur on the 21st of December 2012. But we say that this event is only a half-way point, a tipping point between the old and the new. The ancient structures of the ego will dissolve rapidly. For those unaware, this event could be extremely unnerving and even frightening; it is the responsibility of the awakened ones to comfort and guide them to the light.

Already on Earth, many awakened ones are working in different ways, and by 2012 a vast number of humans will be awakened. But this moment is only the beginning. The work is not done; in fact, it has just started. The real work begins after the Shift, when the masses must be brought out of fear and into the light, and then into the reality of love.

Beloveds, we do not wish to change anything about yourself or your beliefs. We only wish for you to move into that place of boundless joy, peace, bliss, and love that you already are. Ilahinoor is a vehicle of Grace that will open you to the remembrance of your true self, the Great I AM.

Continue your journey wherever it takes you, but bring into your lives the Love and Light of the Supreme. The transformation will happen first on deeper levels, where you may not even notice it, but bit by bit the light will emerge, and the more it emerges, the faster the outer transformations will take place. Follow your truth. We say that Ilahinoor is a gateway, but if that term feels foreign to you, then we say drop it. Call it Divine Light, Divine Grace, Christ Light, Buddha Light, or Cosmic Love. These are only names, and all names are simply a shadow of the Great One, the Self, the Unified Light.

189

Bring this Light into every moment of every day, until you be-come this light. Then your life begins. You will become like a child, always discovering, always curious, filled with excitement at the wonder of life, filled to the brim with overflowing joy, experiencing the deepest peace that has no end. This experience is what you call awakening, or enlightenment. Drink deep the glory of God, sinking deeper and deeper into the vast depths of the cosmic ocean. How can you experience fear in this place? What problems could pos-sibly arise? All is sacred, all is bliss.

I AM the Archangel Gabriel. Ilahinoor Ilahinoor Ilahinoor.

The Ilahinoor Activation

This process came together for me as one means of connecting more deeply with the Ilahinoor field. It is constantly evolving as I evolve — and as I receive feedback from others with whom I work. Take whatever works for you, leave out what doesn't, and feel free to add your own techniques. Beyond any techniques, please re-member that the Grace of Ilahinoor does the work.

The Ilahinoor field is very easy to connect with and to work with. If this is your first time, I would recommend giving yourself several hours to connect with the energy and let it move inside you. Cre-ating a space is important; perhaps create an altar with pictures, flowers, and other sacred objects that bring you into connection with the Divine. If you are doing this practice in a group, perhaps each person can bring something that represents the sacred for them, and create an altar in the center of the circle. Play relaxing music and burn some incense if you wish.

Offer up an opening prayer using your own words — whatever feels right. Decide as a group what you will be doing during the trans-missions. To create a strong connection with the energy, chant Ila-hinoor (*EE LAH' HEE NOOR*) like a mantra. I would recommend that in order to deepen and anchor the energy, everyone receives and gives at least three Ilahinoor transmissions. It builds people's confidence in themselves if they are each willing to give as well as to receive. If you are alone, simply give yourself a transmission.

Invoke the divine to work through you: "Divine Presence, may my hands be your hands, my healing be your healing power, my heart be your heart, and my body be a vehicle for your Grace."

Then, visualize a bright golden light descending through the top of your head, moving down into your heart center, and down your arms into your hands. Wait a few seconds for the energy to flow into your hands, and then start giving the transmission to the recipient. Allow the energy to determine how long to stay in one place before moving on to the next position.

Afterward, share your experiences with the circle, and offer a prayer of gratitude before closing.

You may share this content and process with others. This energy is freely given, and should be freely passed on. It is a gift of Grace.

Deepening into Grace Process

This process will take you quickly and directly to the essence. Each step is a meditation in its own right and can be done separately or all together. It is useful as a daily meditation but you can practice this process as often as you like.

Prelude

Sit comfortably with your spine erect. Close your eyes and focus on the sounds around you. With yourself as the center, listen for sounds around you, as though all of the sounds are coming toward you.

Then, gently bring your focus to your nostrils and focus on the air moving in and out. Pay special attention to the space between each breath, keeping your breath deep and rhythmic.

Notice any thoughts that might pop up, acknowledge them and let them pass through. Continue for approximately five or ten minutes.

Part 1: Self-Inquiry for Contemplation

Hold the following questions in your mind. It is not necessary to find an answer. If answers arise, simply go back to the question. Hold each question until it feels right to move on. If the mind gets busy, move to the next question.

- Is this body mine? Am I sure it is?
- Are these thoughts mine? Am I sure they are?
- Is this mind mine? Can I know this for sure?
- Is this person who I am? Is the personality just a concept?
- Am I more than what I have been conditioned into believing?
- Who am I?

Part 2: Power Affirmations

Make each of these affirmations three times. Start the first affirmation with a focus on the root chakra, and move up the chakras with each new affirmation. The final affirmation unifies all chakras within the Golden Heart. The I AM statements in this section refer to the I AM that is the Divine Self.

- I AM Life. Yes, I AM
- I AM Abundance, Wealth, and Prosperity. Yes, I AM
- I AM All Power, Strong, and Graceful. Yes, I AM
- I AM Healthy, Vibrant, and Harmonious. Yes, I AM
- I AM Divine Will in Action. Yes, I AM
- I AM Absolute, Aware, and Alert. Yes, I AM
- I AM Existence, Consciousness, and Bliss. Yes, I AM
- I AM Love. Yes, I AM

Part 3: Empower the Affirmations with Ilahinoor and the Violet Flame

This section combines two of the most powerful vibrations and energies at this time, the Violet Consuming Flame brought to us by the Ascended Master Saint Germain and the tranquil yet powerful Golden Ilahinoor Grace.

The Violet Flame is the divine alchemical power that transmutes and transforms all the earthly karma we have created and that is held within our personal as well as collective human consciousness at this time. You can bring the Violet Fire into any situation or any emotion, problem, or challenge and change it. The Violet Fire is very effective when combined with power affirmations.

The Golden Ilahinoor Grace will enlighten your consciousness and assist in embodying the Higher Self into daily consciousness, raising us out of the conditioned thinking mind into Oneness.

- Invoke The Divine or any Angels, Guides, Gurus, or Ascended Masters that are sacred and dear to you.
- Visualize a Violet Flame entering into the crown of your head and into the brain. If you wish, you can slowly move your attention through the pineal gland, pituitary gland, limbic system, midbrain, and outer hemispheres, ultimately creating a deep violet halo around your head and leaving your entire brain consumed by the Violet Flame.
- Gradually move the Violet Flame into the entire body, working through the central nervous system, and into each organ of the body. Focus particularly on the heart, lungs, thymus, liver, spleen, stomach, intestines, colon, bladder, kidney, and the reproductive organs. Move into the blood, cells, tissue, bones, and any problematic area. Ask it to move into and between each atom and molecule.
- Then, move the Violet Flame into the subtle bodies (etheric body, emotional body, and mental body) until the whole aura is a consuming violet flame.
- See yourself ablaze with this sacred Violet Fire, as if you were sitting in a deep violet consuming bonfire.

- Ask for it to transmute everything that no longer serves you and to transform all lower frequency fear-based energy, such as stuck habits, addictions, physical problems, insecurities, and so forth into a higher vibrational, expanded state of Love and Light.

- Then, invoke the golden liquid light of Ilahinoor. You may chant Ilahinoor three times if you wish. Visualize this golden light moving through the entire body just as you did earlier with the consuming Violet Flame.

- Pick one cell, perhaps in your heart or in the pineal gland, and call it your Mother Cell. Move the Ilahinoor light into the DNA/RNA of this cell, then ask it to activate your original blueprint, the multidimensional blueprint of your soul.

- Ask the Ilahinoor light to activate the power affirmations within your consciousness, and within your heart, mind, and body.

- Energize it. See the Light getting brighter and brighter, until it is blinding even to the inner eye, brighter than even the Sun. You may consciously say the word *Energize* with conviction three times.

- Activate it. Ask the Light to awaken you. You may consciously say the word *Activate* with conviction three times.

- Anchor it. Become the Light. You may consciously say the word *Anchor* with conviction three times. Affirm your identity with the Sacred Fire: "I Am Light, Yes I AM."

Once you have created this high vibrational space, you can go through your life, choosing whatever you wish to manifest as an expression of your soul destiny. Give each manifestation the individual focus and attention it deserves, visualizing it as having already happened. What would your life look like if you were living this NOW? Offer thanks and gratitude for this divine gift.

chapter 32

The Shaman's Journey

by Sophia Clemenceau

Sophia is a therapist and shamanic healer in the south of France, and can be reached through her website, Spirituel.com.

It is the Spring of 2008, my first meeting with the ILAHINOOR energy! Such beautiful and strong feelings! Sometimes I experience a state of grace, feeling so much in contact with the Source, with the Heavens. Sometimes I contact aspects of my own multidimensionality. As I touch this energy, I understand very deeply what it means to be connected with all forms of life, the spirits of animals, trees, stones, and earth...

A few days after I finished Kiara's seminar in France, I was leading an Elders Lodge, and sharing this energy with people as we prayed and meditated for four days and nights. One morning, as I did an Ilahinoor session on myself, I entered a deep state of meditation.

I am swimming with whales, I am a whale. I am singing with them, their song is caressing my energy. I am breathing with them; we are ONE with Mother Earth. We are breathing together, whales, Mother Earth, and I.

The energy is circulating in my body and activating my DNA. A snake arrives. Little by little, the whale is taking the form of a big turtle. The snake is coiling up on her shell. As he uncoils, he is standing up straight toward Heaven and I feel myself taken all the way up. All this is happening very quickly. I am in a pyramid of crystal and then on Mount Shasta. I meet a White Being; he has a head-dress with flowers. I feel the Presence of Light Masters:

feminine vibrations on my left side and masculine vibrations on my right side. I see a Door in front of me, and they invite me across. As I cross, I find myself in a space of Pure Light, Pure Love. I see the White Being ascending up to Heaven, along with a multitude of other beings.

I feel myself totally immersed in a Love Bath. I am Love. Rivers of happiness are running through me, and I feel so grateful for the Grace of this Gift! My wings are unfurling. I am embracing Mother Earth and all her children. I radiate this Love Energy. I know I am more than human, I know we are all more than human! Most of the time we restrict ourselves, but when we open the Door... WHAOUH!!!!!!!!!!! EVERYTHING IS POSSIBLE!!!

Mother Earth asks me to receive a healing session through the Ilahinoor activation, so I ask a friend to do a session with me. My connection with Mother Earth deepens. I get the feeling that Mother Earth is receiving this session through my body. How is this possible? I see that I am experiencing Mother Earth in my own cells. I feel her suffering but also how strong she is, how much Love she is sharing, and how determined she is in this time of big change!

She speaks through my voice. Her words are coming from very far away. I have a big exhausting feeling, but she is not exhausted. This feeling is the expression of *the end of a cycle*, she is saying. She invites us to move with her. I feel how ready she is for this time. The time is now.

Thank you Mother Earth, I am so grateful to you, I love you so much!

I would say that with the Ilahinoor vibration, I have been able to experience more of my multidimensionality. Little by little, I have been integrating these aspects into my physical life. Connecting with this morphogenetic field helps me in my sessions with clients to connect with a deeper guidance and to assist in the healing journey.

I find that Ilahinoor can be easily combined with other techniques. When I call on the Ilahinoor field, whatever I am doing is quicker, more efficient, and more powerful! Whether doing rituals, medicine wheel ceremonies, or shamanic dreaming, I notice that participants are able to stop their minds and be more present to their experience. In these times of rapid change, Ilahinoor is a very precious Divine Gift!

If each of us could reintegrate our personal being, the Earth would return to balance and peace. This realization is one of my biggest wishes. I dedicate this work to all of my relatives, for the next seven generations!

chapter 33

Manifesting the Light Body

by Karin Batliner

Karin is a shamanic healer and also teaches at a primary school in Switzerland. She is the mother of two children, and can be reached at karinbatliner@gmx.net.

I met Kiara for the first time in March 2009 in Zurich, where he had come directly from Egypt to give an introductory workshop. The first time I received Ilahinoor and sensed the column of light between my hands, I became as tall as a giant — several meters tall. The back of my head was elongated and I didn't feel like my normal self. Several hours later, I was still walking around Zurich with this feeling of being so tall, believing I had to duck whenever I walked through a doorway.

The following night, I dreamt I was lying in a closed coffin. It was dark and I couldn't move because my body was embalmed. I realized that I was lying in a sarcophagus and must be dead. This experience scared me, and I woke up. This dream reoccurred many times over until finally, after several months, my heart exploded in the dream. I burst through the sarcophagus and was free. These dreams were preparing me for what followed, and I was ready.

One morning in the autumn of 2009, I woke up, got out of bed, and could only see bright light. Shortly after this experience, I lost my sense of hearing and asked my daughter to call an ambulance. Then, I couldn't breathe. Fully conscious and with an indescribable feeling of joy, I sat down in a chair in the living room and felt very alive, gigantic, and full of light. I was one with the Ilahinoor field and wasn't afraid, although I couldn't breathe.

Twenty minutes later the ambulance arrived, and the paramedics discovered that I had almost no blood pressure and that my heart was beating only very slowly (like a "hibernating hedgehog"). They gave me an injection of heart medication, after which I could breathe and hear again, but my eyes continued to see only light. It took an entire day before I could see the world normally again; however, the feeling of endless joy and the sense of being taller than normal remained with me for a long time.

On a retreat with Kiara in April 2010, I fell into this state again during a meditation and landed once more in the sarcophagus. This time Kiara was there and helped me go through the process. Suddenly, I sensed my light body and at the same time felt very light in weight. The Ilahinoor field was strongly present and the sarcophagus lid started to become transparent — all the molecules appeared as dancing lights — and I was able to penetrate the lid with my light body.

Looking up, I saw my own column of light, visible through all dimensions, connecting me to the Source. This experience took place shortly before Kiara returned to Egypt. It was clear to me then that I had to go with him, and so I began looking forward to actually lying in the sarcophagus in the Great Pyramid of Cheops. But when I finally got there, I felt directed to lie on the floor in the middle of the King's Chamber and was led through a further process by light beings. Thus, I missed the sarcophagus, but it no longer seemed to be an issue.

These intensive experiences have a direct connection with my life story. They have brought about unbelievable healing and release from childhood traumas, where I had had several near-death experiences related to suffocation. At that time my body was regularly shaken by bad cases of bronchitis accompanied by very high fever, and due to the constricted bronchia, I couldn't breathe. This panic in the face of shortness of breath has haunted me my entire life. Now I am panic free.

Impact on my Life

On the physical level, I've become more stable. Earlier, I continually confronted various kinds of physical ailments. Thanks to the treatments I give myself daily, all these problems have disappeared. I am seldom tired and can deal with the turbulent life of my family much better. I am a very emotional person, and strong emotions have often impaired my sense of well-being. Now I am very grateful to have become more balanced and stable. Whenever I sense that I am beginning to lose my balance, I immediately imagine myself in the column of light and feel the heaven-earth connection. This feeling has been a great help to me.

Strong waves of energy often pulse through my body, usually at night. When this occurs, I can't sleep for hours, but in the morning I'm not tired. However, when this first started happening, I was very dizzy until my brain adapted to the strong waves of energy.

My ability to make decisions is improving, and self-doubt, which has followed me like a constant shadow, is dissolving. I feel aligned with my soul and cradled in light. During this past year, my life has changed completely; nothing is like it was before. For many years, I had prayed for certain things to change, but I didn't have the courage to act. Now it is as though I have begun a new life in my old body.

All this change has also set new processes into motion in my personal environment. My children, friends, and relatives are all being carried along by this wave. When I look back, I cannot rationally understand what has taken place, yet I am filled with so much gratitude for this precious gift.

The intensive transformation this past year has had a lot to do with the fact that I give myself a treatment every morning. Through this regular practice, the bridge from the subconscious to the higher consciousness — to the soul — is always active, and a restructuring of the brain functioning has taken place. This presence is very important to achieving a lasting effect when releasing old patterns. So I'll continue to give myself an Ilahinoor treatment every morning, if only as a way to appreciate my body — and because it's good for me.

I love treating other people and often combine the Ilahinoor treatment with crystals, voice, and shamanistic healing work. It has been a smooth transition and I no longer feel any separation.

My Perception of the Ilahinoor Field

The morphogenetic field, Ilahinoor, is for me an energy of development and growth. When I work with the Ilahinoor field, I feel a strong heaven-earth connection and feel the energy flow in both directions through my body. My connection with this field helps me to manifest my soul's potential in matter. Paradoxically, it feels like I am *on the way home*. For me, being home means ascension to my true being and, at the same time, descension of the cosmic light into my body. It means merging the physical body with the light body. All illusions of separation are removed, the veil of forgetting is lifted, and the divine human can be born. One day, I'll be in full consciousness of what I always was and will be; now I can only guess; however, something in me has always known. This *something* drives me forward and has a vision of the manifested light being who, in truth, I am.

For my entire life, I had the feeling of being a stranger here, of not belonging. I love nature and animals, but I have been afraid of people. It was as though I were an alien floating my way though life just above the Earth. An undefined fear kept me from accepting the Earth as my home. I loved leaving my body and longed for the stars and paradise. During my youth, I was constantly ill and tried to leave the Earth.

The Ilahinoor field and its currents of ascending and descending energies have taken away my fear. Much joy in living on and with the Earth and a deep love and respect for our great Mother Earth can now unfold. I was never afraid of death but rather had great fear of revealing the essence of my being. I preferred hiding with my gifts and treasures for half a century in a cave; now, because I feel supported and anchored in my column of light, I dare to open these treasures without fear, feeling at one with the cosmic light.

Impact on my Work

Now I can travel through the dimensions in full consciousness, without illness, and find my way back to my body alone, without any help. I feel the connection to light beings as I had earlier in my childhood and receive valuable teachings and information from them. This connection is a wonderful and precious gift from the Ilahinoor field.

It is essential that I actively enter into contact, again and again, with the energy — while working, in conversations, on the phone, and when writing and reading — so that every thought, feeling, and action gradually comes to stand in the consciousness of the heaven-earth relationship.

This manifestation, of course, demands a certain amount of discipline on my part. Old thought and behavior patterns continue to reappear and block the flow of light. But I've noticed that recognizing the traps and getting out of the patterns has become easier and faster. I have trained myself to immediately visualize the column of light and anchor it in the Earth whenever I fall into a trap. Then I breathe in and out through the central canal in my back and feel the heaven-earth connection. After this experience, I can release the attachment to the old pattern.

Through the daily treatment I give myself, I gain the necessary strength for the day and am grounded. I have developed a short method for gathering and centering energy:

First, I make the connection between the unconscious and the higher consciousness, the column of light, the connection with the heart, and the little finger on the third eye, as usual.

Then, left hand on back of neck — right hand on left hip, right hand on back of neck — left hand on right hip, both hands crossed on hips.

At the same time, I visualize a pyramid pointing toward heaven Then, left hand on tailbone — right hand on left shoulder, right hand on tailbone — left hand on right shoulder, both hands crossed on shoulders

At the same time, I visualize a pyramid pointing into the Earth.

Both pyramids together form a star.

Finally, I lay a hand (either left or right) on my solar plexus and raise the other hand toward heaven, allowing light to flow into my solar plexus. Then, I place my raised hand on my heart chakra and connect the solar plexus with my heart.

This type of treatment also activates the *Merkaba*.

Being Grounded

I've gained important insight about the Ilahinoor field regarding the subject of being grounded. For many years, therapists have tried to make it clear to me that I needed to be more grounded.

They gave me every kind of advice possible to do so. But no matter how often I tried to sink my roots into the Earth, I seemed to fail. Since I've been working with the Ilahinoor field, I've noticed that I have to take another route in order to ground myself. My way is via the Source. Now I start by opening my crown chakra and asking for a connection between the Source and my soul. The light first flows through my body and then I can anchor it in the Earth. Then I am grounded.

The treatment with Ilahinoor is based on the idea of the column of light anchored in the Earth. Also the Kundalini (which is awakened during treatment by pointing the little finger at the third eye) descends from the cosmic light and is then anchored in the Earth, after which the Earth Kundalini begins to resonate and rise upward. When both energies are in balance, the person experiencing this is in harmony. I still lose my connection to the Source in times of Earth turbulence, but I can restore the connection with an Ilahinoor treatment, which is why I've become more stable physically, emotionally, and mentally.

Even as a child, the Bible verse "My kingdom is not of this world"[1] had already made a deep impression on me and protected me; now, I feel it is so. I am in this world but not of this world. I am a cosmic being in resonance with Earth. From this perspective, I feel fully connected to my Source, which enables me to enter the Earth plane without sinking in the earthly mud. My fear is gone. It's as though I've plugged my lamp into an electric current so that my light can freely shine on Earth.

Ilahinoor and my Dog

Not long ago my dog, Chandra, dug a few nonfood items out of the garbage and gulped them down, which created a block in her intestines. She stopped eating and drinking and finally I had to take her to the animal clinic. After looking at the x-rays, the team of vets wanted to operate right away. But because she was completely dehydrated, she needed an infusion first, and the surgery had to be postponed until early the next morning. I phoned three other women who are Ilahinoor practitioners, and that evening the four of us sent Ilahinoor to Chandra.

The surgery was cancelled the following morning, and the vets began talking about a *miracle*. The clumps had moved down closer to her lower intestine and Chandra was eating again. I was able to bring her home and a day later the clumps were completely passed out. None of the vets could understand how a blockage like this could resolve itself without their help!

chapter 34

Attuning to All Life

by Janice Geiser

Born in California, Janice is a translator and teaches English in Aarau, Switzerland. She can be reached at janice.geiser@sunrise.ch.

———o———

First Experiences

I was introduced to Ilahinoor in March 2009 by my close friend Karin Batliner, shortly after she had attended her first workshop with Kiara in Zurich, Switzerland. She was very excited about this new energy and what she had experienced in Zurich and was eager to share it with me.

I had practiced Reiki several years before, so I expected something similar. She gave me the Basic Treatment and, although I was definitely open to it, I was a little disappointed. I didn't feel any heat or tingling, and because my eyes were closed, I wasn't always aware of what she was doing. The treatment was relaxing and pleasant, but I wasn't sure it had any other effect.

Karin continued to treat me over the next few months, giving me the Basic Treatment whenever we got together. Eventually, I became more sensitive to the energy, which behaved differently from Reiki and could not be anticipated. I became convinced that Ilahinoor was truly having an effect when I began noticing that I was making decisions and following through on them much faster than normal.

A very mundane idea brought this realization home to me. One morning, I noticed a watch I had inherited lying in my closet. I used to enjoy wearing it but hadn't worn it in years. Suddenly the idea of buying a new watchband, but a different color, popped into my mind. It would be like having a brand-new watch! I felt happy as I imagined wearing it again.

The next afternoon I went into town. My first stop was the watch counter at a department store. I intended to just look at their watchband selection and see if anything appealed to me, but to my surprise I left about fifteen minutes later with a new watchband and my "brand-new" old watch! Before Ilahinoor, I would have recognized this kind of "nonessential" idea as good, but might not have acted on it for months — or even years! I am very pleased to report that this was not just a one-time event in my life; I'm now following through on new ideas and decisions *much* faster than before Ilahinoor.

Distance Ilahinoor

From March until summer 2009, Karin attended every workshop she could, learning as much about Ilahinoor as possible without losing her teaching job. Early in July, she organized the first of two training workshops for her friends. It was exciting for all of us attending to finally learn how to give the Basic Treatment. We went home and started treating family members, friends, pets, and ourselves. The timing was perfect for me. I had a couple of weeks to practice before I got the news that one of my sisters in California had been involved in a freak accident, resulting in a badly broken leg. She was scheduled for surgery and wouldn't be able to return to her apartment for several months.

Fortunately, Karin had instructed me on how to send distance Ilahinoor, which I started sending immediately, using my husband as a willing surrogate. Meanwhile, my sister was confined to a hotel near the hospital and was being cared for by friends as she waited for the surgery. The evening before her surgery was very hectic, with people dropping in, but no one could stay long to talk and help her relax.

I phoned her just before she went to bed. She said she was feeling nervous about the anesthesia and possible complications. I told her I planned to send her a distance treatment before her surgery in the morning. I hung up and hoped she could get some sleep. A few hours later, with my husband acting as a surrogate, we sent her distance Ilahinoor at about 3:30 a.m. her time. The surgery went well, but it wasn't until sometime later that I had a chance to ask her if she'd experienced anything special the night before surgery. She reported that she had slept well and hadn't been aware of any physical sensations between 3:30 and 4:00 a.m; however, she recalled having a dream that comforted her and helped her trust that the surgery was going to be all right: She had dreamt that both her legs were covered with water lilies and the water lilies were gently massaging them!

I continued sending my sister distance Ilahinoor over the next several weeks. One time, I was with Karin, and we sent Ilahinoor together. Before we began, we held hands and invited my sister to join us. Karin suggested we wait until we both sensed a sign to proceed. Karin saw a pink light, and I felt a warm glow of love in my heart. Then, with me acting as the surrogate, we sent my sister distance Ilahinoor. I emailed her, letting her know about the distance treatment she had received and mentioned the two signs. To my amazement, she emailed back and told me her favorite color was a fuchsia pink and attached a photo to illustrate. The flower in the photo was exactly the same color Karin had seen!

Shortly after my sister's surgery, something similar happened as my husband and I were preparing to send her Ilahinoor. We were holding hands, connecting through our eyes, and silently inviting her to join us. Suddenly I sensed her energetic presence so strongly, I could have sworn she was standing next to me on my right! I don't recall what, if anything, my sister consciously experienced during that treatment, but I will never forget her energetic visit direct from California to our living room in Switzerland!

Reports from People I've Treated

Over the past year-and-a-half, I have treated people privately, in workshops, and in our monthly Ilahinoor meetings. I love to hear anything people wish to share about their experience, because — as I learned right from the start — the effects of Ilahinoor can't be anticipated. During the treatment, people usually appear relaxed — even to the point of falling asleep. But the relaxed state can be deceptive. After some of the treatments, I learned that a few clients had been shown pictures of a past life, which they could then connect to their present life.

In one session, a client alternated between diving deep into the ocean and flying in the sky — she loved it and didn't want to come back! One went on an ocean journey and recognized herself as a leading member of a whale pod. People suffering physically often experience Ilahinoor energy moving through their bodies, clearing out tension and softening their defensive body armor, making it easier to release whatever is causing pain.

I find it amazing how even one session can make such a positive difference in a person's health and emotional well-being. I knew I was onto something powerful when, after her first Ilahinoor treatment, an energy practitioner opened her eyes and said, "Wow! I've never experienced anything like that!" Recently, an Ilahinoor practitioner whom I treat, told me matter-of-factly: "Ilahinoor is a safe and pleasant way to have an out-of-body experience." We both laughed, but I thought that those words summed it up neatly for many people I've treated so far.

chapter 35

From the Egocentric to the Divine

by Kirstin Dennis

Kirstin is a beautifully aware healer living in close proximity to several megalithic sites in the south of England. She can be reached at kirstin@lyncholt.co.uk.

———○———

I used to be normal. I did all the things a normal person would do. I never questioned any of it. I was a busy salesperson having a successful career. I was a mother with a busy family life and a loving husband. I knew what was expected of me. I knew how to keep my life ticking comfortably. I was safe.

This situation all changed during my first summer of visiting crop circles. Until then, I had believed the media story that all crop circles were man-made hoaxes; however they are made, crop circles are beautiful, peaceful places to visit, where people of all backgrounds, including what the mainstream would consider "wacky," can meet.

During one of these crop circle visits, I met an interesting looking group of people — Kiara among them — in the stunning *Owl* formation of 2009. I was immediately interested when I heard them talking about healing energy and wanted to learn more. A lovely lady named Sarah offered to give me a hands-on demonstration of the Ilahinoor energy they were talking about, which I eagerly accepted.

I had never experienced any kind of healing energy before. Amidst the dust and noise of the combine harvester getting closer and closer to our magical oasis of woven wheat, I received such a wonderfully powerful Ilahinoor transmission that I was transported to a lush meadow filled with wildflowers beside a beautiful mountain stream. I found myself in tears, and when I opened my eyes had the sense that my eyesight, hearing, and other senses had dramatically improved!

From then on, Ilahinoor has stayed with me. It somehow seems to transmute any negative situation or blind spot I may be experiencing, either by magnifying it so that I can see more clearly, or by clearing out subconscious blockages or conditioning.

The first time Ilahinoor became very active for me, I was meditating with *chakra music* under a beech tree at sunset. My entire body began vibrating with an immensely strong energy never experienced before. I was not able to move for an entire forty-five minutes, and it left me baffled but very excited. Looking back, I now understand this experience as a sort of clearing of my neural pathways, a surge of cleansing, beautiful energy flowing into all the cells of my body as it descended from the cosmos down through me into Mother Earth.

My next encounter of a similar kind occurred during a crystal workshop while lying down inside a crystal array, taking part in a guided meditation. At this stage in my life, I was spending time every day teaching myself to see auras by letting my eyes go soft, and letting my peripheral vision take over. I could only ever see a faint haze around plants, animals, and people — nothing like the full-blown aura that you read about in textbooks!

So there I was on the floor, the crystals amplifying the fine Ilahinoor vibration that I was experiencing at the time. This vibration increased until it was nearly as strong as when I had done my sunset meditation. As the energies coursed through my body, I happened to think of my mother in Germany. Immediately, I had a vision of her surrounded by the most beautiful gold, turquoise, and green colors! I do not know where this vision came from — all I knew was that I had never seen anything like it before. I then thought of my sister, and a vision of her in different colors played before my inner eye. The same experience happened with every person I thought about! Ilahinoor had enhanced my earlier attempts to see auras to the point that I could see vivid colors around people. It was lovely!

In the times that followed, I continued to experience gentle vibrations throughout my body, generally when I was in beautiful surroundings, or when I spent time with people who moved me. It was as if Ilahinoor was guiding me to seek out these surroundings or people.

We are probably all aware that within a group of like-minded individuals, energy exchanges are much stronger, and that during energy healing workshops, we often achieve unique insights. Such phenomena continued to happen to me, and during one Ilahinoor workshop, I gave Reiki and Ilahinoor to a lady who was feeling quite depleted. While I worked, I suddenly began to see her chakras. Her throat chakra glowed red, so I gave it extra healing. It turned out that this lady had a thyroid condition! I was moving rapidly along the path to being a healer!

During the two years that followed, I began to experience subtle changes in my perceptions of life, and a more questioning attitude to things I had taken for granted. I was gaining a *helicopter-style* overview of things, where I could lift myself out of my current dramas to see the bigger picture. I became aware of how interwoven we are with each other and the world around us. I began to experience a greater element of synchronicity, mostly in the form of inspirational books or people who came into my life, always at exactly the right time.

Not only did I awaken to the interpersonal relationships of humanity, but I also became very acutely aware of all life forms on Mother Earth. I always had a loving relationship with animals, but now this bond extended to plants, too. I recognized the living being in each plant, each with its own healing essence.

One day, as I wondered what it must feel like to be a tree, the energy started to flow and I simply became one! In my mind's eye, my arms were ancient branches with golden-green leaves absorbing the Sun's energy. I had a sensation of photosynthesizing the Sun's rays with my leaves, and felt a strong surge of energy coursing up my trunk while being deeply grounded and anchored in the Earth. My legs and feet had become a very complex root system. It was amazing!

With all these beautiful experiences, however, was an aspect of my journey that was not so easy. I had made many new friends during workshops and meditation groups, but with regard to my family life, especially my long-suffering husband, Antony, life had become difficult. I had changed. I no longer identified with many of the typical issues and problems of day-to-day family life. My priorities no longer matched those around me. Yes, I was still functioning within the family, but it was not my only focus. Antony began to feel neglected and lonely, believing he no longer had my support.

Antony was very understanding, and never tried to hold me back from what I needed to do, but it was not easy for him to deal with my changed attitudes toward him and the things that were important to him. We did not seem to have much common ground anymore. The more I tried to involve and "convert" Antony toward my world of spirituality, the more I pushed him away. We started to argue. Deep down, we knew that we still loved each other, and I longed for a more loving relationship with my husband. I had heard about *spiritual lovemaking*, but we had never experienced such a close connection — and now it seemed to be slipping totally beyond my grasp!

Here, again, Ilahinoor wonderfully obliged. I was at an Ilahinoor workshop with Kiara, in a beautiful safe caring environment, and was doing an exchange with a very gentle, deep, and caring man to whom I had felt instinctively drawn. As my partner, Matthew, (not his real name) gave me Ilahinoor, I had an astonishing, life-changing experience.

As I entered a state of energy vibrating and humming within, I suddenly sensed myself surrounded by a love so deep, so strong, and so eternally pure that it felt almost physical. As the transmission ended, I leaned into Matthew, and we stayed like this for a long time, feeling like it was the most natural thing to do. This was the closest I had ever come to spiritual lovemaking, and I told Matthew so. All conventions appeared to have fallen away in this deep state of love. In this timeless moment, I also realized that I had known Matthew for a long, long time. I saw and remembered us together in previous life times, living a spiritual life as medicine man and woman amongst Native American Indians.

This experience was so amazing for me that I felt compelled to contact Matthew once I got back home. It felt both reassuring and unsettling to realize that Matthew had experienced the same wave of love. We struggled to explain to ourselves and to each other what had happened. I did not know how to discuss this feeling with Antony, but instead found myself increasingly turning to Matthew when I felt low, or when I needed a soulful conversation. Each contact gave me a boost, and I felt myself being held in a beautiful love. At last, here was somebody I could open up to, someone with whom I could share my innermost thoughts.

At times, the bond between us was so strong that we did not need words or phone calls to communicate; it was based on a link of pure psychic nature. Were we experiencing true Oneness, perhaps? I had started to live life very intensely, surrounded by love, soaring like a hot air balloon across the sky.

Although Matthew and I were communicating regularly, at no time did we deem this new association to threaten our respective marriages. We felt instinctively that this connection was of a different kind, best described perhaps as a meeting of soul mates. It was not meant to lead into anything else. Our precious connection was simply enriching us, and infusing everything we did with love.

Over the next couple of months, this bond became very important to me, and I must admit that it was clearly me, of the two of us, who was the needy one in the relationship. It was always me seeking answers and receiving advice on all sorts of matters from my newly found, spiritually advanced, and well-balanced soul brother.

The whole Matthew experience was enhancing my life in a beautiful and wonderful way. The feelings of love and freedom I was experiencing actually made me feel much closer to Antony also, and my love for him grew. But because this experience was all happening during an intensely busy time in our family life, we were still rather distant. Antony was working sixteen-hour days on a huge renovation project for our future, and he certainly didn't have the time or mental capacity to understand what was happening to me.

For the most part, I did not feel any guilt about what I was sharing with Matthew. I had not done anything wrong in the conventional sense. There was nothing physical in my relationship with him, and this new feeling of love improved my whole life. What could be wrong with that? Also, everything felt very innocent, especially because our shared experience had happened within the sacred energy of Ilahinoor. I was very grateful that Ilahinoor had shown me such love.

However, it had also thrown me into deep turmoil, and highlighted very strongly the incongruity between my husband and myself. What's more, I still had not found a way to explain to Antony what had happened, and something had started to feel very wrong, because I was keeping the source of my altered existence secret from him. My life was starting to feel a little schizophrenic, and I wished for an opportunity for things to come out into the open.

To make a long story short, Antony came across some of my emails with Matthew one day, which showed quite clearly the spiritual intimacy we shared. In his mind, we were having a spiritual love affair, which was even more hurtful than a sexual one. At least the latter can often be explained in terms of lust: this one was far deeper and therefore more painful. Here was another man who exhibited a spirituality and sensitivity that allowed him to connect with me on a deeper level than he, my own husband, could himself. He felt betrayed and utterly devastated.

My own response to this discovery was different. I felt a huge sense of relief that things were out in the open. I felt that this sudden shock would bring him back to me emotionally; force him to listen, to understand, to realize what had been missing. Whereas he felt like our marriage was over, for my part I could see that now, finally, we had the chance to build something new and stronger together.

What happened over the following two months is a bit of a blur. At first, I just could not see Antony's point of view. I had a sense of righteousness, because deep down I really did not think I had done anything wrong; nor did I feel as terrible about what had happened as Antony expected me to — which, in his eyes, was adding insult to injury. But I could see the pain that my perspective was causing, and slowly began to understand how he must be feeling. While maintaining a sense of detachment from the drama, I began to feel a pure love and compassion for my husband.

Very slowly, the situation started to improve. I made it clear to Antony that I did not want to end our marriage; I loved him and wanted to stay with him. As the pain started to subside, Antony began to understand and believe what I was saying. We spent a lot of special time together, trying to repair some of the long-term problems that had developed during our years of marriage, and were rebuilding our relationship.

Both Antony and Matthew had been wonderfully supportive when things came out into the open. Once Matthew understood that Antony felt hurt by the depth of our connection, he gently withdrew, not wishing to cause further pain. But Matthew had become my spiritual lifeline, and with this withdrawal my beautiful balloon came crashing down to Earth. I lost the feeling of being fully alive. I felt that in order to support Antony, I would need to deny the spiritual lifeline I felt with Matthew. The support did not originate with my husband, and was therefore not allowed within our society.

How we limit ourselves! In order to keep Antony, must I never feel any other love? What was this love that I felt in the first place? It was not a personal love but a part of myself, and the loss of this love felt like a great gaping wound. In order not to hurt Antony, I was no longer able to be truly myself; I could not feel or express all that I was. Something within all this felt so wrong, so conditional, but I could not really understand why and what. It was so much greater than just the loss of occasionally talking with Matthew.

Help came in the form of a book called *Wild Love* by Gill Edwards, which was recommended to me at exactly the right time by my highly intuitive Reiki teacher. It describes the difference between conditional and unconditional love. Antony read the book from cover to cover, and began to really understand how we imprison and tame our partner when we can only love them conditionally, which is of course what we are all taught to do in a conventional marriage.

This realization helped him to see my connection with Matthew in a new light. He began to understand the free spirit of human beings, and with the new closeness that had developed between us, he was led to feel much more open and less threatened by my spiritual path — and the people I might meet and love along the way. He realized that he could free himself up as well, do more things in his life, and share his wonderful openness and zest for life with other people of either gender. We were starting to turn the corner onto a beautiful road where we no longer felt so trapped by the egotistical emotions we were expected to feel according to the strange conventions of our modern world.

Six months on, we are still travelling along this road. We now know where we are going, and we are both totally committed to going there together. From my perspective, it is like I have a new husband. Our experiences with Matthew, the *Wild Love* book, and the week that Antony and I spent at a highly transformative Tantra festival have brought us closer than I ever dreamed we could be. Our relationship is now beautifully open and honest, and I can talk to him about absolutely anything. He has been able to replace what Matthew brought to my life, and a whole lot more.

I know many spiritual women whose husbands want absolutely nothing to do with spirituality. I am very lucky that Antony has a beautifully open mind, and is able to connect with his deeper self. I believe in my husband, and I am convinced that together we can support each other to develop this infinite love that can free us from the illusion of separation.

I'd love to say that it has all been smooth sailing, but that would be far from the truth. In being so open and honest with each other, Antony and I have had to deal with all of our ego-based emotions as they come along. It sometimes feels like a crazy rollercoaster ride! But as each situation arises, we know we can deal with it, and it's easier each time around. We are slowly but surely moving toward a truly beautiful way of being together.

I know that we would never have been in this process of finding a much deeper love, if Ilahinoor had not intervened in my life. So it is with optimism for the future that I conclude the current stage of my journey with Ilahinoor. It is a journey about finding and connecting with my true self — which is pure love — and to integrate it into my life here on Earth. It is sometimes tortuous and painful. But who said a visit to planet Earth would be easy?

chapter 36

The Sacred Feminine

by Kathleen Landbeck

Born in Chicago, Kathleen is a homeopath and Gestalt therapist living up in the mountains of northern Italy. She can be reached at k.landbeck@gmx.de or through her website, My-self-care.de

My journey with Ilahinoor began just a few weeks ago, but it has taken me further than any fantasy I was ever capable of dreaming up. Ilahinoor has blessed me with uncountable magical moments.

My neighbor here in this mountain village in Italy told me that she was expecting a visitor — a healer and shaman — and that's how I first met Kiara. He was travelling through Europe, giving lectures and teaching about how to tap into a divine energy he calls Ilahinoor. I was immediately touched by what he was sharing.

That night I dreamt that the most beautiful man came to me with this question: How can a man show a woman that he truly loves her? While I answered him, I realized that he wasn't asking me because he wanted to know theoretically. He loved *me* and wanted to know how he could show me his love! I woke up feeling totally, unconditionally loved. I was beaming! My body was streaming with heat and energy. My heart felt bigger than the house I lived in.

I felt I had to share this dream with Kiara the next morning. He asked me what my dream response had been. I told him: A man shows his love for a woman by acknowledging and worshipping her true womanhood and by his willingness to learn from her.

What exactly *is* true womanhood? Unfortunately, many of us don't have a clue. I myself had in past years just begun to get a glimpse of understanding! Back in the 1970s, I was a feminist, and loved working and being with women. But many of us were more caught up in fighting male chauvinism than in discovering ourselves and living true womanhood. Many of us had forgotten our intuition, our nurturing talent, our ability to connect and communicate deeply, our oneness with nature and mother Earth, expressed by the cyclic physiology of our bodies, our strength and ability to endure pain when necessary, our receptiveness and emotionality, our psychic powers, our ability to heal, and — most importantly — our ability to birth!

Dearest sisters, our deepest inner resources are desperately need-ed on this Earth. Our western civilization needs our wisdom, and our men need to share in our true womanhood. The state of our economy, our environment, our Earth depends on this sharing. So a man who loves a woman will acknowledge and value her true womanhood, and will also understand that he needs to learn from her.

He will not fear her. He will not abuse her in order to feel stronger and more powerful. He will not reduce her to a sex object. He will not try to own her. He will cherish her, do everything in his power to keep her safe, listen to her, be passionate *and* compassionate with her. He will support her inner growth and not feel the need to compete with her. He will rejoice in her strength and rest in her arms. Once there, he will find a haven where he can be all that he truly is, where he can put down his masks, shields, and swords, where he can rest and rejuvenate, be held and healed by her. Both people will give up control, paving the way to passion, ecstasy, and oneness. How can our men acknowledge our womanhood if we ourselves fail to do so?

The next day, Kiara gave me the manuscript of his book *Year Zero: Time of the Great Shift.* During the next two days, I could not stop reading. If I had seen this book on a book shelf a month earlier, I would have rolled my eyes and thought, my goodness, another doomsday story that feeds on our fears. But, as he spoke of how these global changes were serving the evolution of humanity, I was fascinated. Kiara doesn't preach in his book. He shares his knowledge, convictions, and experiences, and simply invites us to join him in making this world a more loving, compassionate place to live. What a wonderful invitation!

I felt hope — a feeling that confused me at first. I had been trying to make a difference on this Earth for years. Since I was a young girl, I had been politically active, working for ecology and peace movements, for justice in our educational and police systems, for the rights of minorities and refugees. Everywhere I went, a job seemed to be waiting for me. After the events of 9/11, I felt overwhelmed and exhausted. I seriously questioned whether our efforts over the years had made any difference at all. I changed my strategy, and decided to simply focus on myself, address my inner wars, my own hates, prejudices, and fears. I decided it wasn't worth engaging in a futile attempt to change the world, when I no longer felt any such hope existed.

Hope, I had learned, was a trap that keeps us from being fully here in the moment. How often had I, years before, settled for less, put off being happy, held on to dysfunctional relationships or unhealthy habits because I hoped something would change, some day, somehow?

Kiara's book talked about the enormous changes going on in our galaxy that were affecting our Earth, about the Maya calendar, about a pending evolutionary leap of consciousness. Reading the book left me with a feeling that I had purposely not nurtured for many years. But why?

Suppose we assume that everything we hope for is already here, a true part of our living reality. What if our absolute and relative realities exist hand in hand, two sides of the same coin? Then, hope is not escapism, but perhaps a glimpse of a bigger living truth yet to be unveiled. As I read Kiara's description of the radical events and changes moving toward us at a very face pace — but also of the opportunity we will have to evolve into a more loving compassionate human species — I cried. How I longed for this! Dare I hope? Could he be right?

I attended his Ilahinoor seminar in Zurich a few days later. It was a joy to witness the unpretentious, loving way he got his message across to his audience, and how he touched so many hearts. I found it easy to tune into this energy. It felt so strong and vibrant, and went right through me as if no physical boundaries existed. Everything seemed to quiver in me and around me. The atmosphere was warm and open hearted. When it was my turn to give Ilahinoor, it didn't feel new at all! I was completely relaxed and had great trust in this energy.

Much happened in the two weeks that followed, even though I spent most of my time immobilized on my bed on the balcony. I had been out hiking and had fallen, hurting my knee quite badly. But somehow I felt very safe and cared for. Although it was in a lot of pain, my body just would not accept any pain medicine. Since I received Ilahinoor, my body had begun to change and my taste buds were revolting against even my favorite foods like gelato and cappuccino! Many days I could only eat fruit. I was sleeping much less, waking up in the wee hours, even before the birds. I used the time to write, to meditate, and to listen to my heart.

The hours between four and eight became a special time in which my Ilahinoor journey would intensify. As my dream had shown me, I was feeling a strong desire to transform my personal relationships into a greater love. I knew what didn't work! But how do we learn to love? My experience with Ilahinoor was soon to awaken in my heart this long forgotten knowledge!

Wouldn't it be helpful if we had a handbook that helped free us from the emotional traps of possessiveness, manipulation, aggression, and jealousy, all of which are based on feelings of being unworthy and unloved — something that could help us stay not just emotionally well balanced, but mentally and physically healthy as well? Well, I am convinced that the Ilahinoor field is this living handbook. Touching this field was like sinking into a bubble bath of pure love. I was reminded once again what I had learned through a message that came to me in meditation over a year before:

You are lovable, a jewel, a wonder, a divine creation, a loving and creative expression of the eternal consciousness. You have succeeded in finding the path that leads to me. Your bravery is admirable and you are full of love and compassion. Be careful with yourself. Keep your willingness to learn and to embrace your shadows. You need not be perfect in order to be lovable. Just relax, and be as you are in this very second. It is not necessary to add or take anything away.

You can depend on me. I will always be there for you when you need me. You have come a long way. You can rest and take all the time you need. Relax and take good care of yourself. When you continue on your path, go slowly and with awareness, step by step. Take your time and everything will happen spontaneously. You are a daughter of God. You are love and you are welcome on this Earth. You are my daughter and I will take care of you. You are not alone. You are in the right place at the right time. Feel my embrace and let your trust grow. You are almost at your destination and have an infinite amount of time.

Yes, indeed! We are creations of love, but who was this Creator? I had no idea that the answer to this question was waiting for me right around the corner.

I had signed up for a retreat in Germany with Kiara for the first week in July. I could still hardly walk due to the pain in my injured knee. My neighbors had to help me down the steep pathway to my car, carrying my luggage for me. I got in the car, but on a sudden impulse decided to leave my crutches behind. I still believed, however, that my first stop after the seminar would be the orthopedic doctor.

After my first session with Ilahinoor at the retreat, the pain in my knee was about 60% better. Every day afterward, it continued to heal and, by the end of the five-day retreat, I was completely pain free! The night before leaving I was actually dancing!

A still bigger discovery came during the shamanic breathwork session, during which we were blindfolded. The journey I took over the next two hours was an important stepping stone on my journey of awakening. I found myself in the galaxy, out among the stars. I saw the Earth from this cosmic perspective, and all the pain that was troubling her. I saw the pollution, the wars, the oppression, the rape, the hunger. I felt such great love for her.

I gently removed our suffering Earth from her orbit, took her into my arms, and cradled her like a baby. I softly asked her, "How could you have doubted me? I would never let you fail! Don't you know how much I love you?" Then, I slowly pushed Earth into my abdomen and birthed her anew. And there she was, a new Earth, healed and radiant. I was in awe! I put her back into her orbit, and just continued to adore her from above, awed by her beauty. Physically, I could feel in my pelvis the after pains of birth. It felt sore, but there was so much joy seeing my beloved Earth in her full potential — her full glory!

Then, my breathing stopped. It was fine. I didn't care in the least. At a certain point Kiara came and touched my heart. I took a first breath once again. It felt as if I had been under water too long and I gasped for air as I finally made it to the surface to fill my lungs again. With this breath, I went flying through the cosmos at great speed. I just kept going and going and going. It was soon clear that there was no end, ever! Great laughter arose from me. Distance and the time didn't play a role any more. I was everywhere and nowhere. I had birthed a new Earth out of love. I was love. I was a creation of love and I was the creator of love. I was cosmic consciousness.

The next day, as we did a healing circle, we placed pictures and names of people in need of healing in the middle of the inner circle. I experienced very strange sensations in both of my hands. They were electrified. As I looked at them, they felt somehow strange, not really belonging to me. I could feel them being "rewired," and the energy emitting from them was strong. I knew I could heal with them and stretched out my hands to hover over a picture of a participant's son who was struggling with burn-out. I was so grateful and touched by the transformation of my hands!

For me, these bodily sensations and changes were important, for they were a sign that I was really integrating what was happening to me. Our minds are tricky and our egos are very creative! But the wisdom of our bodies is totally honest. I have learned to depend on that wisdom and to be guided by it.

In the weeks that followed, I grew more and more grateful to be on this Earth, here and now. I truly was in the right place at the right time. Now I am so very happy to be able to share this journey with you.

These six weeks changed me, changed my life. Kiara once told me that perhaps my years on the mountain were a cocooning. I think he was right. I have a freedom now that seems to exceed all of my dreams. My intuition has been sharpened, I feel deeply relaxed, and I have learned how to heal in a new way. I no longer feel that desperate need to make this world a better place to live in. Yes, I will continue to help where there is a job to be done, but I know that I am no longer the *doer*, just a part of an infinitely intelligent and loving cosmic consciousness. In this I trust.

For me, it is not an accident that Ilahinoor attracts so many women. Birthing is in a woman's nature and we have a job to do! It is time to transform ourselves and to create a new Earth. We can't do it alone, however! In my heart, I know that on the new Earth women will once again fully embrace their true womanhood and this act will help all men and all women develop the human potential needed to create and live in loving, caring synergy with our great Mother Earth. I look forward to seeing each of you there!

chapter 37

Rediscovering My Inner Light

by Lila Heart

Lila is a writer and psychologist from Holland who enjoys travelling the world. She can be reached at Lila.AwakenedHeart@gmail.com.

My Life a Few Months Prior to Ilahinoor

Before I met Kiara for the first time, I had heard stories about his being an incredibly enlightened man. Perhaps it's my rebellious attitude, or perhaps it's my unique perspective as a young woman, but that didn't particularly thrill me. I had never been a seeker of enlightenment, whatever that meant, and I wasn't looking for any kind of *guru*.

Instead of a guru, however, I found an old friend. At that time in my life, I had been feeling immensely tired and depleted of energy. It was a trying time — everything was shifting and I seemed to be experiencing a Dark Night of the Soul. I can't recall when exactly it happened, but I abruptly awoke from this dream called Life and began questioning everything around me. Nothing seemed the same anymore, and everything I had ever believed in seemed to be shattering in front of me. Even my closest friends had become strangers. It's like I never knew them. And if I didn't even know my closest friends, how was I supposed to tell what's real and what's not?

My bubble burst when I started asking myself if I was really happy. I felt like my whole life had become one big responsibility. Even being happy felt like a responsibility. I couldn't bear to grimace even when I was having a rough day because too many people depended on me. Ever so slowly, I had slipped into a web of burdens, putting everyone but myself first. I didn't even recognize this change until everything started falling apart.

It wasn't anything spectacular, just a slow creeping realization, until suddenly the world wasn't the same anymore. When I found that I was too tired even to get out of bed, I knew I couldn't fool myself anymore. I was stuck in a cobweb of illusions and conditioning, continually attracting experiences into my life that were shaking my belief system to the core. The very foundations of my life were crumbling, exposing all the rot underneath. I didn't know what was true anymore, but desperately clung to what was familiar.

It was in this state of fatigue and fragmentation that I heard about Kiara, who was doing a workshop close to where I lived. I hadn't read his book and knew nothing about him — just that he worked with this energy field called Ilahinoor. Feeling depleted, and desperately needing an energy boost, I decided to go. I figured that anything that could raise my energy would be welcome. I had no expectations, but went with an open mind, ready to let the Universe unfold in front of me.

It's not about gurus or enlightenment but about finding our Light within.

I was curious about meeting Kiara — and if he really was what people had told me. My first impression of him was that he was an ordinary man, which surprised me in a positive way. Was it me, or did he seem just like everyone else? At that point, rreferences to gurus didn't strike me as particularly positive. My reason for feeling this way was that often gurus are seen as highly evolved and enlightened beings with a great deal of knowledge, which is all fine except that many students who are seeking gurus become dependent on them and never learn to find the universal truths and knowledge within themselves. I've even seen gurus who say to their students that only *they* can heal them or bring them to enlightenment.

Our journey on Earth is about freeing ourselves and more fully embodying our True Presence. I could never accept that other human beings could tell me they are better than me, for in God's eyes or Source or Universe, we are all equal. And even though not all gurus are like that, a great deal seem to be. So my resistance to that whole image is deeply rooted within my being and has propelled me to find the Truth deep within myself — and not to look so much to others for answers.

That's why I found with great joy that Kiara is just a normal human being, just like me, just like everyone else. There's no pretense or trying to make himself out to be something more than he is. And I liked this honesty and realness about him; I appreciated how he encouraged people to find their own Light instead of becoming dependent on him and seeing him as some all-knowing guru. And this self-reliance is what Ilahinoor is about: finding your own Divine Presence, and realizing that it has always been there. It's about anchoring your own Light, your Soul or Higher Self, within your physical body — and living from that Space of Love.

Ilahinoor is about realizing your higher potential and letting your actions stem from the infinite Source within. This feeling is what we desire most, it is what many search for when searching for enlightenment. But if we are projecting this feeling outside of us, putting someone on a pedestal and worshipping him or her, continuously depending on others for answers, how can we find this Light within? How long until we realize that the gurus we look to for answers are simply reflections of ourselves?

We never walk this journey alone; we will likely turn to others for assistance at times. Yet this support does not mean we should rely on them forever. Like baby birds, we are supposed to spread our wings and fly. And, in return, we acknowledge and show gratitude to those who've reminded us that we can fly when we've so miserably forgotten. We find a great humility when acknowledging those who have helped us become aware of our own Source of Light, instead of becoming dependent on them and surrendering ourselves in a helpless fashion until salvation comes.

This knowledge is what Ilahinoor is about for me. It's about empowerment, not submission; it's about taking responsibility for ourselves and becoming aware of our own Light.

Life after Ilahinoor

Ilahinoor has helped me become aware of this Inner Light, of the Universal Source of Love that fuels my existence. It has empowered me and allowed me to experience a deeper awareness in my daily life. I am much more grounded and hopeful, so that now I can successfully master this life instead of seeking to escape it.

The first time I experienced Ilahinoor, I was surprised by how strong yet gentle it is. I have worked with several energy systems but have never experienced an energy that was strong yet soft. It amazed me how much power exists within this softness. It is the power of Love, gentle but strong, an unconditional love, a divine power that nourished me.

In the weeks following my first experiences with Ilahinoor, the same issues I had been dealing with before reemerged; but this time they dissolved. What made a great difference was that even though I continued to feel my personality disintegrating, I could now surrender to it. I became aware of the forces that worked with me and through me — of which I had earlier been unaware. I became much more aware of the fears that held me back, and my resistance to the process of healing and embodying my Soul Presence.

I realized that I had lost a big part of myself in trying to identify with the illusions of this world. This realization had already been happening prior to Ilahinoor. But now, as I could let go of my conditioned identity, I was starting to rediscover my true self. I could go through this process of letting go with grace and composure. Instead of clinging to everything I had ever known, I let go and drifted off into the vast magnitude of the Unknown.

When I re-emerged I felt different. My state of mind had changed; my mode of thinking was altered. I didn't think in terms of problems but in terms of possibilities. I entered into a more continuous state of awareness and observation without the need to judge between wrong or right, and without much effort to maintain this state.

At first, I fluctuated wildly. I would lose my awareness and become disconnected with my soul, then awareness would come and I would find my way back. Since then, it's become effortless, and I find myself in a more or less continuous state of awareness.

I still practice Ilahinoor regularly and have to say it has altered my life. It has unleashed a dormant potential within me. For me, the personal experiences with Ilahinoor have not been as important as the shift in consciousness that has occurred in a short period of time. The more I am willing to surrender to the universal flow of life, the more rapidly these changes are manifesting themselves through me and in my life.

I believe these changes in consciousness can happen much easier with the aid of Ilahinoor, but it is up to us to surrender to the Infinite Source of Knowledge within, the part of us that knows us better than our personal egos ever will. Ilahinoor is a guide, helping to dissolve the conditioning and fears that keep us from surrendering to our Divinity, the Inner Flame.

We can liberate ourselves from our hurt, sadness, pain, and anger that we have learned to carry within, and which we often refuse to acknowledge — for fear of rekindling a deeper, buried pain. With the awareness and acceptance that Ilahinoor brings, this process can occur naturally and with ease. And as we clear our pain and heal our hearts, we can make room for our True Selves, our Divine Selves.

chapter 38

Dying into Life

by Franz Ilah Loibner

Ilah is a wonderful spiritual therapist, healer, and artist who lives near Graz, Austria. He can be reached through his website: Ilah.at.

———◇———

My experiences with Ilahinoor go back several years — actually to the beginning of Kiara's rediscovery of this divine force — and continue to grow. It always amazes and humbles me to feel the infinitely grand cosmic support we are given for our awakening process. I have been using Ilahinoor to increase my consciousness and to heal myself. I have used it with other people, and also with animals. I have worked with Ilahinoor in group retreats and seminars. The high vibrating divine energy of Ilahinoor has also been extremely helpful in my Lomi Lomi treatments and in my care with terminally ill people.

My own path of awakening has been shaped and assisted by a number of wonderful experiences. I feel less and less attached to any sense of a personal self; rather, I feel ever more strongly that the cosmic currents unite us all. To my mind, this feeling is not only due to my own desire to let go and surrender, but also to the growing morphogenetic field of descending light that is shaping our collective destiny.

Through the grace of Ilahinoor, I am more and more capable of experiencing this feeling of unity, this deep emotion of being connected to everything and to everybody, this oneness with all that exists, this indivisibility of the internal and the external, the inseparability of you and me. You and my own self: They are no longer distinguishable from one another.

A few years ago, when my ego spoke louder than it does today, I believed that it was I who possessed healing powers. Nowadays, I recognize that healing happens in the high vibrating field of Ilahinoor, which simply allows the person seeking help to better mobilize his or her self-healing potential.

An aunt of mine, for example, was diagnosed with terminal cancer and imminent organ failure. The doctors gave her only twenty-four or forty-eight hours to live. After an Ilahinoor treatment — with remote group support by Kiara — she was released from the hospital completely cured, and free from any cancerous tumors.

Working in groups is particularly strong because it amplifies the Ilahinoor field. Feedback from participants covers the whole range from visions of light to experiences of oneness, from feelings of bliss to absolute speechlessness. In groups, it is usually not so relevant whether you *receive* or *give* Ilahinoor... it is only important to be surrounded by this field and to be permeated by it, right down to every cell within and beyond the physical body.

Neither is it about holding any particular Ilahinoor points, but rather to be fully present and let the energy do the work. These external positions are helpful when you first start experimenting with Ilahinoor, but after a while these become less important than the ability to simply connect and hold the field of light. For example, when making a Lomi Lomi treatment, I can make use of the high-frequency Ilahinoor energy without any bodily contact, even over vast distances, without any loss of intensity.

One of my most beautiful experiences with Ilahinoor was in accompanying my father on his last earthly journey. Over a period of more than a year, I was privileged to hold the Ilahinoor points while washing and bathing him.

My father was not a spiritual person in the classic sense, but as he was able to open himself more and more to this experience, he became increasingly calm, and more and more prepared to leave. In the last days of his earthly life, he gave us the present of his incredible willingness to accept this transition that we call death; until his very last heartbeat, he let us share his magical and miraculous passage.

The grace to accept his dying so fully, and at the same time to share this journey with his closest relatives so beautifully, was without any doubt strongly supported by the frequent Ilahinoor energetic work. Quite often I accompany dying people during their last days and hours, and always feel touched and enriched by the energies that become active during this process of transformation. Held within the field of Ilahinoor, surrounded by the scent of fragrant oils and delicate incenses, I find that accompanying a dying person through this gateway of death is always an indescribably beautiful experience.

Apart from these special occasions in which it can be very helpful, Ilahinoor supports those who are ready to open their hearts to the magnificent transformation taking place on Mother Earth today. The energy of Ilahinoor, fully available to all, is a great help in carrying us through situations of anxiety and fear, when we wish to cling to what feels safe and familiar, failing to recognize that change can be beneficial.

I have been in the Great Pyramid in Egypt, and I have gone swimming with whales and dolphins in the open seas. These experiences for me were very similar to what I have experienced in the field of Ilahinoor. From the depths of my heart, I thank Kiara for helping us remember who we are, so that we can allow ourselves to be carried from separation back to oneness.

The energy of Ilahinoor is not the only way to make us aware of our essence and our divinity, but it is a beautiful and graceful way to evolve. May Ilahinoor nourish and accompany you on your journey back Home.

chapter 39

Within One Moment

by Tara Birgit Schallek

Tara is a shaman and Earth healer from Vienna, Austria. She is often on the road and can be reached at Tara.Green@gmx.net.

———◇———

It all happened within one moment. Kiara sat in front of a man and started to build up the soul-to-soul connection by looking into his eyes. He wanted to show us how Ilahinoor works. And it worked. Oh, yes. Within one moment, all happened. I could see the transpersonal chakra fields above the man's head being activated. The global or planetary chakra field, the galactic chakra field, and, on the top, a chakra field I have never seen before but somehow know. I just have no name for it.

And what I saw was just beautiful and amazing. I could feel how the man's heart opened up and was filled with all this amazing light. And then I could see the Merkaba turning around but also being stabilized in a way. It all happened actually within one moment of time. And I sat there pretending only to watch, but at the same time realizing that all of us sitting around were part of this process.

Kiara went on helping to integrate what could be integrated. I understood that the procedure that followed was an integration process, so that one is able to feel and so to experience what actually already happened. The point is to open up the Ilahinoor field. Ilahinoor is part of our consciousness and when you focus on it, an amazing potential opens up. So Ilahinoor is one of the bridges to our potential. It is one of the tools we have been given for these times and, on the other hand, it is timeless. It is a gift that only works when you go into your heart where the bridge starts.

Later on, when I worked with Ilahinoor I experienced the love of the *Elohim*. I could see Elohim energies surrounding us like columns of light. Some people told me that they had never experienced such a strong love. And this love opened their hearts; sometimes it even felt like an explosion so that they could feel eternity within seconds. And when they opened their eyes again, I could see this light flickering in their eyes.

I understand that *giving Ilahinoor* means working as a channel for these energies, which also means receiving all this wonderful light. And so I just simply let it flow, not trying to want anything, not trying to heal or to be a healer. This experience has nothing to do with me as a person. Ilahinoor can work with each person according to his or her unique needs. We all have our experiences, our own jobs to do here on this wonderful planet called Earth, and so not everyone has to experience the same things. But one things stays: the feeling of deep inner peace and LOVE.

For me, Ilahinoor is a bridge for peacefully walking over into my potential. I have felt many of my old patterns dissolving. These patterns may be useful until we reach a stage of consciousness where we are ready to integrate and incarnate more; but then they are no longer needed. And the one giving Ilahinoor is also the one helping you to integrate, building up a field of pure love, where you can easily take what is already a part of you.

For me, this one was Kiara and I am glad that it was him. Other people were pretending just to sit around, but holding this strong field so that I was able to take my steps. Thank you all! You made it happen.

So whenever I get the impulse to work within the Ilahinoor field, I just follow this impulse, knowing that I am just a channel that has experienced the power myself.

Ilahinoor is always just a thought away and as soon as I think of it, it is there; or, I am there.

chapter 40

In Resonance with Divine Love

by Dini Visser

Dini is a TM practitioner, music teacher, and Deeksha giver living in Lelystad, Holland, and can be reached through her website, Ilahinoor.nl.

———o———

Some events in life make such a deep impression upon us that we know we have to find out what is behind them. Such an event happened in November 2004, when I met Kiara and Grace for the first time. They were giving Deeksha transmissions then, and there was so much love being transmitted, I found myself unable to look into their eyes. It was just too intense for my body, even though I had practiced Transcendental Meditation for almost thirty years. Afterward, I found myself held in a deep transcendent state that lasted for hours, and only gradually diminished in the days thereafter.

I told myself that I needed to find out more about this energy. I followed their Deeksha transmissions for many years and, in August 2005, I became a Deeksha giver as well. But then suddenly in 2006, Kiara introduced a new energy that had come to him in Turkey — he called it Ilahinoor.

It felt nice and more grounding to bring the energy deeper into the physical structure, especially when Ilahinoor was combined with Deeksha. But this work was still in its infancy then, and I have noticed over the years how it has grown and developed into the strong, solid, full-grown energy it is now, able to penetrate into even deeper levels of our physical existence — as if each new application has opened the gate for integrating this energy even deeper. And, over the years, it has felt like the morphogenetic field of this energy itself has grown stronger, thus allowing new people to more immediately have the same profound experiences.

Ilahinoor, although strong in itself, is easily combined with other modalities, including Deeksha. I remember in the very beginnings of my Ilahinoor practice, a long-term Deeksha giver expressed her astonishment about how powerful this Ilahinoor energy felt for her. And here are the words of another person after receiving her first Ilahinoor session in a weekend course where we exchanged Ilahinoor: "Wow, this is the best thing we ever did until now."

Recently someone told me that she had started a new job in which she at first did not feel at ease. All the new things coming to her made her feel uncertain, fearful, and too wound up to sleep at nights. Then she decided to give herself Ilahinoor after work and now she really likes it. The job is the same, she said, but she herself feels totally at ease again.

The beauty of it is that these kinds of experiences are happening even when people practice it on each other for the very first time. There is no need to go through an expensive or hierarchy-based initiation before being allowed to share it with others. The energy of Ilahinoor is simply available for everyone who is willing to open to this morphogenetic field and everyone is allowed to teach it to someone else; no hierarchy, no other person between...

For me, these three pillars — the TM-sidhi program, along with Deeksha and Ilahinoor — are a beautiful garden of flowers enhancing and sustaining each other, opening my heart deeper and deeper to the wonder of life. I have gradually learned to release my fears of sharing what is real for me, even when I know that others may disagree. I have learned to accept my dreams as potential truths instead of pushing them away as unrealistic, for what is life other than this potential for making our dreams come true? But above all, I have learned again the real meaning of the word *Love*.

It is not always easy to live in a world in which we are often raised to deny our inner world as unrealistic, a world in which the word *Love* is so often misused for something it is not. Still, deep inside we all need this Love so much. All life is simply an expression of Love; *WE* are Pure Love in our deepest essence.

Once we have experienced this *Love*, then our journey of life can begin in a new way, guided by a deep longing for wholeness that stirs within our hearts. Nature starts to help and guide us more and more: We are in the right place at the right time with the right people so that we can give and receive gifts and guidance from the Universe.

Every morning just after awakening, I practice Ilahinoor on myself, lying in bed for as long as my body needs, allowing this energy to bathe my body in light. I describe here an experience I had in July 2007, in which I underwent a rapid shift, from deeply held anger to intense harmony, followed by a strong feeling of Oneness and Love.

Waking up at 6.00 in the morning, I had planned to do some Ilahinoor and then go out to do my TM program in the dome. But I fell asleep again and woke up much later with the experience of a big wave of anger coming up inside me. Raging inside, I decided to do some Ilahinoor work to harmonize.

Suddenly, it was as if a blanket of very soft light was laid over me, consisting of a dense web of very tiny particles of light, soothing, loving, peaceful, immediately dissolving all resistance and anger. It felt so good to lie silently embedded in this web of harmony that even moving to another position felt disturbing.

I found myself in a deep state of Presence, feeling at one with whichever people in my life I decided to focus my attention on. I felt a soft light and love flowing through me, causing my body to weep intensely as deep hidden pains were released from the cells of my body.

Just when I'd think it was over and make an attempt to sit up, new waves of energy would flood through me, and the story repeated itself, over and over. And even when I finally got out of bed and went on with my day, it continued — waves of this intense Love flooding through the cells, freeing blockages, freeing the breath, and freeing the heart.

At a certain moment, when I experienced again this deep union on the level of my heart, a very special, strong, solid energy started to move through my whole body, filling it, opening the cells, feeling totally surrounded by it. Perhaps there was more space created now for my higher presence to enter my body.

During a time when Kiara and Grace had gone to the Red Sea with a group of people to experience swimming with dolphins, I had the following experience, which highlighted for me the connection between Ilahinoor and these beautiful cetacean beings.

For three days, I experienced how intensive dolphin energy waves were sweeping through my body, making it alternately laugh in ecstatic happiness and cry in a kind of sadness. One time it went on for an entire afternoon. There was a moment that I felt myself swimming skin to skin with a dolphin, our bodies moving in synchronicity. Another time, I experienced being surrounded by a circle of dolphins. The next day, still lying in Ilahinoor position in bed, I experienced ecstatic love-waves again sweeping through my body.

A New Addition

New additions to the Ilahinoor work seem to pop up when the time is right. Some are probably only meant for our own personal use at a particular time to help clear a specific blockage. But sometimes it can be useful for others as well, and I would like to share one position I have been experimenting with in the hope that it can help people in their process.

While lying in bed practicing Ilahinoor one day, after doing the Ila-hinoor bridge and the heart activation, I found myself making a connection between the Ilahinoor points in the back of the head with the solar plexus region, which suddenly created a strong reaction in that area. I went on and completed the session, as I normally would, but felt this moment was somehow a missing link, allowing the light to enter into a denser physical level of the body. It caused in me a kind of cellular joy, which stayed that entire morning.

Practicing it on myself and others in the weeks afterwards, I became aware that it can bring up some strong stuff, not only physically but also emotionally. It is a powerful position, but should perhaps be used with caution, depending on the readiness of the person receiving. It is also possible to use this solar plexus position with the hands slightly away from the body rather than by physically touching.

I have also used this position with people during a rapid eye movement session with good results. With one client, whose issue was loneliness, she started with an intensity of 9 (on a scale of 1 to 10). After working for some time, it went down to 2. When I asked where it was located in her body, she placed her hands on the heart and stomach.

So after doing a rapid eye movement session, I started with the Ilahinoor bridge and heart activation, and then placed my hand a little out from the solar plexus with one hand while holding the Ilahinoor points with the other.

As I expected, this position first activated the intensity of her feelings up to 5, but after further rounds of the rapid eye movement, she suddenly started laughing and went all the way down to 1. Afterward, as we exchanged places and she began to work with me, the same thing happened with me. I felt a rush of Kundalini through my spine, and experienced a complete clearing out as well.

On another day, when lots of unpleasant things were happening in my head, placing my hands in this position gave me a feeling of soothing relaxation and balance. So this position can create activation as well as balance. It feels like an important addition to the sequence when done with caution and care.

In summary, exchanging Ilahinoor with people has been a beautiful gift for me. It is the energy of pure unconditional love, bringing us into resonance with the Divine Source. Ilahinoor is a huge gift to humanity, and I am grateful to Kiara and the Ilahinoor guides for sharing it!

chapter 41

Ilahinoor and Deeksha

by Aurelia Taylor

Aurelia, along with her husband, Al, works with a wide variety of healing modalities, including Deeksha and Ilahinoor. It may be that the experiences shared here will be helpful for other Deeksha givers wishing to combine these two streams of transmission. Aurelia lives in Denver, Colorado and can be reached at aureliatara@aol.com.

I am hesitant to believe that there is only one flavor to divinity as it expresses itself on Earth, and so I love trying new and diverse ways to help bring those energies in for humanity's expansion and growth. Ilahinoor provides yet another avenue for seekers to experience that loving oneness.

Ilahinoor feels very feminine and nurturing in its expression, and truly IS divinity in action. Because our groups all love Ilahinoor so much and find it integrating and grounding, I would definitely tend to believe it is helping to anchor the new cosmic energies that are coming into Gaia. As represented by the symbolism of the Star of David, Ilahinoor is divinity merging with form. I love saying the word, *Ilahinoor*. It honors another aspect of the Divine through the Turkish tongue and certainly pays tribute to that part of the world as a result!

Ann and Donna are Deeksha givers, and always conduct Ilahinoor transmission at each of their events. They always ask people to share experiences afterward and we almost always have people sharing about Ilahinoor and the sweetness, softness, gentle touch that they experience. Too bad I didn't take notes over the years, or you would have a book full of testimonials. But here are a few:

245

I'm *Donna Baldwin*. I first experienced Ilahinoor quite a few years ago when I received it over the phone from Kiara. I felt the energy and really got excited about it. Then I heard about it from two Deeksha givers in Oregon and how it helped them integrate the Deeksha energies. So I called Ann Hines, who was a blessing giver working with me. I asked her and husband, Bill, to come over and gave it to them, as suggested on Kiara's web site.

Bill immediately felt the energy, even as I was talking and explaining it to him. So we started giving it after our Deeksha events. We'd take a little break and then end with sharing Ilahinoor. We explained it was to help ground and integrate the Deeksha energy. I've always experienced it as a soft, feminine energy and we love it and use it and share it at all our events now!

My name is *Bill Hines*. I was introduced to Ilahinoor by Donna Baldwin. The moment she sat down and started to talk about Ilahinoor, having said Ilahinoor just once, I felt an infusion of very strong profound energy, different from most energies I feel when I am meditating. As Donna continued and guided me through the initiation, it felt like a wonderful new energy that I would enjoy experiencing time and again in the future. For me personally, the energy is a magnetic frequency that is very soothing and grounding.

My name is *Alicia Ponce* and the Deeksha and Ilahinoor has created an opening to heal with my mother, who passed over in 1980, and that has allowed me to heal and continues to allow me to heal the rest of my family as well.

My name is *Kathleen Humphreys* and I've been receiving Ilahinoor for three or four years. It is amazing and such a complement to Deeksha. It feels like a soft Divine Mother energy that is very comforting and soothing and encouraging. It's just so lovely... there's just such a sweetness to it and I always feel so calm and peaceful afterward. I really like it. I always like it!!

My name is *Sue* and I've been receiving Ilahinoor for four months. What was so powerful for me the first time was that beyond the fact that the evening was so powerful and just so moving, it continued to build and build for days afterward and just kept opening and opening and opening things for me. My mother passed away within a couple weeks of my first experience, and I feel that having these experiences with Ilahinoor helped me be much more centered through her passage. It's been such a blessing!

My name is *Paul Barney-El* and I've been a healer for several years. The Ilahinoor was very interesting and I received it several times. After one experience, I felt something break loose. Tears started coming; that was different but it was things I needed to release. Of course you don't come to a public venue and say, "Oh, I need to release this and that, but so it snows." It was wonderful... awesome!

My name is *Cynthia Farley* and I've been an energy worker for quite some time and I just want to express my gratitude to you for bringing this ability to work with Divine Light back to us again. I felt the experience to be soft, warm, and complete!

My name is *Sandra Gourd*. I find that when we do Ilahinoor after doing Deeksha it is such a soft, loving energy. It's just like icing on the cake. It's just so wonderful, this energy, and the feelings that you experience. I always feel my heart opening. It's definitely a nice addition to the Deeksha experience.

My name is *Shirley Morgan*. The first time I experienced the Ilahinoor energy, it was so incredibly beautiful. Each time I experience it, it continues to be more and more beautiful. To me it feels like such love, such compassion, such grace... it feels like a mother's hug. It just takes my breath away. It is a beautiful, beautiful energy and I am so grateful for it!

chapter 42

Communicating with Animals

by Barbara Maleah Chyska

Maleah is a horse trainer and also teaches classes in animal communication. She lives in Luxembourg, and can be reached at maleah@emoko.net.

My name is Maleah and my life as well as my work is centered around animals. I have practiced intuitive — or so-called telepathic — communication with animals for as long as I can remember.

When I met Kiara some years ago and got to know Ilahinoor, I felt it as a wonderful energy that helped me to change things in myself. I always had the idea of taking this energy to my animal friends and seeing how they liked it and what they thought about it. In this chapter, I would first like to ask one of my best friends and most important teachers, Tom, to express his experiences with Ilahinoor. For those who may wonder, Tom is a seventeen-year-old horse who has given me the honor of living with me for nearly a decade now:

Can you imagine a place where there is love, nothing but love? A love that allows everyone to grow and to become what he or she is meant to be? It is the energy of Ilahinoor. We know it, because it is our way of teaching. Pure unconditional love is the frequency of change on this planet. And Ilahinoor is the same wave, the same power, the same light. This light opens up a space within which any transformation is possible. Even though our bodies can adjust to the changes of our planet more easily, do not forget that we, as parts of human families, help you to carry your emotions.

248

We help you to learn and to transform, so sometimes our bodies also get sort of stuck in lower frequencies. This sometimes leads to quite a lot of pain, especially in the joints and spine. Using Ilahinoor for animals means helping them to help their families. Transformation happens quickly in our bodies and minds. We are not so much attached to matter. Changes are rushing in nowadays, so let's ride the wave together, helping and guiding each other. You just have to tune into the energy and listen, then you will understand and start to see...

A friend of mine once told me that horses are said to be the dolphins of the land. After all the years I have spent with them, learning from them, teaching them, watching them, I believe it. There is a reason why dolphin and horse therapies heal so many people around the world. They are connected to this wave of transformation, to this frequency of love. And when we connect with this frequency, we also connect with their healing powers. My closest friend is my dog, Leah, who is at this moment lying on my bed warming my feet. She once answered my question about why she liked Ilahinoor as follows:

When you practice Ilahinoor I understand you. Normally you try to live your life thinking about everything but not feeling and knowing what has to be done. It is very hard for me to connect with you in this state. But when you are in this energy you are so clear to me. I can understand you, I can feel you. It is so relaxing for me, there is no tension, no stress, and I know it is the same for you. This is how the world is meant to be. Lead by heart and not by brain. Be guided by wisdom and not by what you have learned. This is the teaching of the planet and I love to see you connected, listening to the messages of life itself.

chapter 43

Rivers of Life

by Martina Nergl

Martina is an event organizer and media host living in Erfurt, Germany. She can be reached through her website, Spirit-lounge.com.

—————○—————

"We are all waters of different rivers; that's why it's so easy to meet," said Yoko Ono many decades ago.

If we could see ourselves and our environment from this perspective, many things would be a lot different today. When we look at the world of the twenty-first century, there is still genocide, there is still war, there are still the games of secrecy and power, there is still pollution everywhere, and exploitation of environment resources. There are still millions of people unaware of their inner wisdom and knowledge, while others still do their best to keep a sick system going.

"I know," you might say, "but what exactly can I do about it?" Here is the good news: You are much more powerful than you could ever imagine; and, as you come into an experience of unity within yourself, you can change the world around you. Ilahinoor can help with this effort. In my own practice during the past years, Ilahinoor has helped me become aware of new dimensions of human existence. It has allowed me to be interconnected yet grounded, mentally more open, physically and psychically healthier. My perceptions have changed from doer to doing, from being an actor to being an observer.

This change has made my life easier, allowing me to stay in peace with whatever changes are going on, reminding me to trust my inner power and wisdom in all the actions and decisions I make. And since every single human being is a perfect blueprint of the whole universe, as we change inside, we change the world we are living in. Take one minute every day to remember that we are all water of different rivers, and that all these waters flow into the same ocean. As we meet in this ocean, heart to heart, let us dream a new world awake.

I would like to deeply thank Kiara Windrider for his maternal wisdom, his universal knowledge, and his never-ending efforts to make this world a better place. I appreciate his friendship in this world — and between the worlds.

chapter 44

A Medley of Ilahinoor Experiences

Awake in the Dream

by Catharina Roland (Austria: catharina.roland@gmx.at)

Nina is a documentary filmmaker from Vienna, Austria, who recently produced Awake in the Dream, *a documentary featuring many contemporary spiritual teachers and healers in an exploration of our planetary future. Please check out her website, Awakeinthe-dream.net.*

After reading Kiara Windrider's book on Deeksha, and feeling a desire to meet him, I travelled to Graz for an Ilahinoor workshop. Receiving my first Ilahinoor by Kiara was a pure blessing, and I immediately felt a wave of divine light filling the cells in my body.

But the most astonishing event happened the night after, when I was woken up by an enormously strong and intense wave of energy, which travelled from the top of my head throughout my whole body. I was literally shaken by this strong and loving energy, which filled my cells and shattered the perceptions of my body's limitations. I could feel myself as ONE with everything around me, with EVERYTHING THAT IS. What a divine blessing!

I appreciate Kiara´s work as a cocreator for the New Earth and feel blessed by his friendship, touched by his gentle, soft, and powerful appearance, and very grateful that Kiara is an important part of the creation of the documentary *Awake In The Dream*. Thank you, Kiara, and oceans of love to you!

Opening the Heart
by Gilia van Dienst (Netherlands: gilia@leefjehart.nl)

Ilahinoor is a great help in opening my heart again and again, so that I can feel receptive at all times and have the courage to live fully. When I connect with this field, I experience the world again with wonder and feel much gratitude. Despite being on a spiritual journey for a long time, I have moments when emotions and limiting thoughts affect my happiness. Old trauma and misery get triggered, and I experience myself going into fear. But when I connect with this field, I recognize that these feelings are not real in themselves. It becomes easier to go into my heart and experience the qualities of love, compassion, trust, faith, hope, devotion, life purpose, primal stillness, intuition, courage, creativity, joy, forgiveness, unity, devotion, gratitude, and synchronicity.

When I go into my heart, these qualities flow freely. In order to make this transition out of pain and tightness, I need softness. The enormous energy of Love I experience with Ilahinoor becomes a door into my heart! This feeling allows everything to flow again. I am who I am again — a divine being on an earthly journey. And it is very easy to let Ilahinoor work for me. If I haven't used it for a while, I go through all the steps to open the field. But when I use it regularly, I feel that it starts to flow as soon as my attention goes there.

Ilahinoor is a great way for me to help myself, so I can then teach others to open their hearts. It is the sweetest thing I know how to do!

Ilahinoor and the Innernet
by Corinne van den Eeden (Luxembourg: Corinne.vandeneeden@ education.lu)

For me, Ilahinoor is access to the morphogenetic field of light. And this field is like the *language of the heart*, a language everybody

253

understands somehow: humans, animals, and all living creatures. It is like the language we spoke before we built the tower of Babel. It's a symbol of what we can achieve if we speak the language of the heart.

When Kiara talked about the *innernet* in one of his Ilahinoor workshops, at first I did not understand what it was about. I tried to imagine how it would work; it scared me, too. Would I be able to use this innernet? Two days after the Ilahinoor workshop, I made an astonishing discovery. I sent a short message via my mobile phone to a dear friend of mine. Some minutes later, I heard her answering in my head and saw her answer before my inner eye, like a short message for my head.

It made me smile because I felt the feelings she was sending with this message, too. This entire exchange took about a minute. Ten minutes later, I received her short message on my mobile phone. It was exactly what I had experienced, but without the sound and the feelings. My experience showed me that this innernet did exist, and I knew that when the moment came, I would know how to use it!

Floored by the Light
by Depy Surya Spyratou (Greece: surya_and_pepsi@yahoo.co.uk)

In November 2009, I started reading Kiara's book *Journey into Forever* while in Puttaparthi, India. One day, I took it with me to the German Bakery and was reading it over a cup of coffee. A friend approached, sat at my table, and said to me, "You know, he is coming to Puttaparthi next month and will be staying in the building right next to yours!"

I was amazed, first of all because I found the book so interesting, and secondly because I had never before taken a book to read at the German Bakery. It was obvious that I had done so in order to receive this message and eventually to help plan Kiara's trip!

He arrived in December for a few days only and we quickly managed to arrange an Ilahinoor group at a friend's house. After Kiara gave us an introduction to himself, his work, and the wonder of Ilahinoor in our lives, he called me up to be the first participant in his Ilahinoor demonstration.

We sat opposite each other, looked deep into each other's eyes, and then he placed his hands on my head, one on the forehead and the other near the back of the neck, and held this position for some time. As I sat on the floor, I thought to myself, "What am I going to tell all these people who are now watching me and waiting for me to tell them what is happening? Nothing is happening."

And then, SUDDENLY IT HIT ME!!! I literally felt this enormous energy hitting me, coming into my body from the top of my head. It was SO strong that I couldn't remain seated. I felt dizzy and started rocking back and forth. Kiara helped me to lie down on the floor and there I LAY FOR 45 MINUTES UNABLE TO MOVE. I tried to get up but it was impossible, and every time I tried, waves of nausea forced me back onto the floor.

Another group member who was sitting very close to me was trembling uncontrollably throughout this time.

I could hear everything, but was totally unable to move and lay in a world that seemed very different to the world I had just been in.

For days after this experience, I was flying. Not only was I happier and calmer, but also my so-called "big problems" seemed so much smaller now, my worries became fewer and fewer and everything in my life seemed to flow.

If only we could work with Ilahinoor more, how different our lives would be!

Wonderful Experiences with Ilahinoor
by Arianna Urania Stalder (Switzerland/Malta: raghura@gmx.net)

During Easter 2010, I received with Kiara and friends wonderful gifts of awareness and perception from the spiritual world and the Ilahinoor treatments. Since then I have integrated this Ilahinoor light into my healing treatments, which were among other things I offered for six months at a spiritual training center during the summer and autumn of 2010.

Really wonderful and lasting healings took place there! I would like to describe what happened very simply:

In the first stage of the treatments, while making eye contact (the soul merge), many faces that didn't belong to our present time were shown to me, and I discovered they had to do with past incarnations. These are appearing now, it seems, because the time has come when old, energetically stored charges want to take their leave, charges that had previously been impossible to access.

This experience lasted for different lengths of time, and sometimes faces appeared that looked agonized and tormented, and not very comfortable! When the contours became fuzzy and only violet light appeared, this was a sign to me that the issues were resolved, either for the moment or, in most cases, released for good! Then I could continue, connected with the morphogenetic field and spiritual helpers, working with the guidance I was being given.

The joy and gratitude of the people and the reports of their experiences make me very happy; they give me the assurance that I'm able to make a contribution to the whole, to the growing consciousness here on Planet Earth. Some people made comments like these:

- They felt like they were newborn
- They become aware of old burdens and clearly felt a release
- So much love and warmth
- Feeling of freedom
- Plus lots of positive and loving feedback...

My heart is full of gratitude and love, and I'm happy I am able to contribute to the ascension of willing people.

Ilahinoor and Reiki
by Ewa Jankowska (England: emdmrd@aol.com.uk)

I came across Ilahinoor last year when Kirstin phoned me to see if I would like to come to a course to learn about Ilahinoor. At the time I was looking for something but didn't know exactly what — so, when Kirstin phoned me it seemed like such a synchronicity. The next thing I knew, I was in the course learning all about this amazing energy called Ilahinoor. When I was given a treatment/transmission of Ilahinoor I felt peaceful and nurtured. The energy was so powerful — I was totally amazed.

After the weekend, I was interested to see what would happen to my healing. I run a holistic healing practice and have been working with Reiki energy for over ten years. The healings I have been doing since that weekend have been so much more powerful. My clients have been relaxing more and relaxing much more quickly. The healing that has been happening is amazing. I also feel the energy flowing through me much more powerfully than before. It feels very strong and direct, but at the same time healing and nurturing.

Ilahinoor and Psychotherapy
by Annette Lehmacher (Germany: AnnetteLehmacher@gmx.de)

Whenever people with anxiety problems came to see me, I use Ilahinoor as an additional tool to my work, especially when clients are very activated right in the beginning of a session. I gently interrupt their flood of words and touch them on their heads, building the Ilahinoor bridge and letting the energy flow for a couple of minutes. Afterward, they always sense a remarkable release of stress or anxiety, and we are able to continue the work much more effectively.

Ilahinoor and the Clearing Process
by Melek Mjaanes (Turkey: melekhakyemez@hotmail.com)

Ilahinoor has made a major shift in my life and work. The first time I received it from Kiara, my heart started to pound as I had never experienced before. The strong beating continued for almost a week. I was irritable and needed time for solitude, feeling very vulnerable and out of control. It went down into my solar plexus and pelvis. I had no idea about what to expect and what not to expect. At the end of the week, things started shifting in my life. I had to let go of certain relationships, others transformed.

Issues that had bothered me for some time started either to resolve or to bother me even more, thus pushing me to make internal changes. The effect was like a wave, passing from me on to the others with whom I was in contact. I am extremely grateful for getting to know Kiara and for having Ilahinoor in my life. It is a continuous healing process for us all. We meet once a week on Wednesday evenings in my home and practice Ilahinoor, and just let it emanate!

Treating my Cat
by Renate Fischer (Switzerland: fischerinstrument@bluewin.ch)

I have a British-Blue cat named Sissy. Two years ago, when she was fifteen, Sissy had a slight stroke. When she became active again after a few days, I noticed her dragging her right back paw and limping. So I began giving her Ilahinoor treatments throughout that summer. She visibly enjoyed the treatments and, at the end of the summer, I was happy to see she could walk normally again.

Two weeks ago, shortly before Sissy turned seventeen, I saw her having trouble jumping up onto a chair, and I realized her lower back had given out. Once again, I began treating her, this time every evening. Now, two weeks later, it is much easier for her to move.

I am fully convinced that the Ilahinoor treatments are lightening my cat's twilight years.

A New Energy

by Kimberley Jones (England: kimberleyjones@lightcoaching.co.uk)

As a healer and energy intuitive, I have had broad experience of different energies and healing modalities, and it is quite something for me to encounter an energy that feels at all new or remarkable to my system.

The moment Sarah contacted me about Ilahinoor, I felt something deep in my bones that declared "YES!" As she prepared to share the energy with me, sacredness in the room was tangible. I felt a matrix of support and excited attention surround me as guides, light beings, and pockets of observing consciousness became alert. I could sense something important was happening.

As the transmission continued, I became aware of the left and right sides of my brain dancing with each other and trying to engage with what was going on. Neither side could; that dialogue seemed to be bypassed altogether. This was an exclusively sensory experience. It felt great to let go, to feel my mind letting go of the need to know, and my body letting go of the need to hold.

The energy comforted me deeply throughout the session. I felt safe, held, and deeply nourished.

The hand positions crossing the body prompted the energy to begin moving within me in a particular way. I could feel it. An ascending spiral of energy began moving up my spine; the effects of this motion could be felt through my whole body. Then, a descending spiral began swirling down my spine, intertwining with the ascending spiral. Over this sensory image developed a superimposed layer of something else. Gradually it became clear to me that I was seeing/sensing a DNA helix and being shown the process of my own DNA changing in response to Ilahinoor. I have never consciously experienced this sensation before.

Then I became aware of the stream of Source energy and Earth energy directly entering my system via these spiraling energy channels and portals that had been energized within me. I felt a deep balance and peace within my heart. I could taste the newness and the ancientness of Ilahinoor. I was changed.

Through the Earth Connection was the feeling of a loving mother nurturing me that, along with the Spiritual Father Light that was flowing into me from above, allowed me to feel safe enough to arrive more fully into my body. This experience resulted in some strong feelings in my joints and muscles, that soon passed, but which I enjoyed as confirmation that a deep process of embodiment had accompanied the influx of Light.

This energy feels as natural and simple as the breath. Pure Light and Love is beyond ownership, but I was certainly grateful to receive the blessing of this energy and I look forward to sharing it with others.

Love In My hands

by Caroline Probyn (England: c_probyn@binternet.com)

One of the most astounding effects of Ilahinoor is to so quickly break through and dissolve old patterns; stubborn ingrained resistances to the gentle persuasion of Love's truth, but without needing to delve into reasons or histories — although these may naturally surface, to be washed away in the soft stream of a mother's touch! Ilahinoor is a gift in the truest sense, in that it is given, wholly and completely — not on loan, not half given with strings, attachments, preconditions — but given from the heart to the heart, to be passed on to other hearts.

And the only requirement to give or to receive it is being human, being here, and being willing. There is no teaching to follow, or enlightenment to attain, only the experience of complete, open acceptance of the perfection of Love that we always are and that is always at our disposal.

Ilahinoor has been one of the deepest and most tangible experiences I have had of pure, unconditional love, and the transformations it has brought have entered my heart like waves upon the shore — with the gentle insistence of the dearest and most honest friend.

Ilahinoor is like being cradled again in the arms of your mother. When the going gets bumpy and the Earth beneath your feet feels unsure, she is there and you know you can fall into her Great Love, and be rocked by her gentle words, "Yes, I am here, I am still here for you, it's OK, I'll never leave you!"

This week, when I was getting myself into a typically anxious state about something, my hands automatically and quite unbidden flew up to my chest and rested on my heart and I found myself saying over to myself, "Calm down, it's not important, calm down." In that moment, my hands seemed to belong to someone else, some far more evolved being than I could imagine myself to be at that point in time!

At any rate, there was Love in my hands, even while there was anxiety and fear in my mind and heart, as though my body's own wisdom had overridden my mind at that moment. It was an extraordinary sensation, to be commanded by the part of myself that appears to have moved forward since my meeting with Ilahinoor. It worked — miraculously!

The White Mist
by Sue Rees (England: sue@reesroberts.plus.com)

I asked Spirit to give me some information about Ilahinoor. It showed me a vision of Earth covered in a white "mist" — this, it said, was Ilahinoor. It showed me a chain of people around the world, holding hands. It then showed me the Ilahinoor energy coming into my chest from above, in a sort of funnel shape. Spirit described Ilahinoor as "the light that shines from God," which "causes us to know His acceptance."

A Closing Definition
by Susie Ankhara (England: susieankhara@excite.com)

Ilahinoor is a soft, gentle, and loving energy that has the potential for profound shifts in conscious awareness and understanding. It also has a beautiful balancing and grounding affect on the physical body. Once attuned, the energy is always available and may be called upon at anytime, simply by naming it, or by thought or feeling: "ILAHINOOR."

END NOTES

Chapter 1

1. Kiara Windrider, *Year Zero: Time of the Great Shift* (Boulder, CO: Divine Arts, 2011).
2. Paul LaViolette, *Earth Under Fire: Humanity's Survival of the Ice Age* (Rochester, NY: Bear & Co, 2005).
3. Although there seems to be evidence pointing to a 12,000-year pulse, other researchers are equally convinced that the timing of these pulses corresponds to a 13,000-year cycle or a 11,500-year cycle. It all seems to come down to the length of the precessional cycle, which is calculated in different ways by different people at different times. I am not so attached to the exact length of these cycles, as there is a wide enough range in geological data so that the same data can fit both models. I do feel, however, that we are in a transition zone between cycles, whatever their precise periodicity may be.
4. Douglas Vogt, *God's Day of Judgment: The Real Cause of Global Warming* (Bellevue, WA: Vector, 2008).

Chapter 2

1. Robert W. Felix, *Magnetic Reversals and Evolutionary Leaps: The True Origin of Species* (Bellevue, WA: Sugerhouse, 2009).

Chapter 3

1. See article on <http://modernsurvivalblog.com/pole-shift-2/alarming-noaa-data-rapid-pole-shift/>
2. Talk by Don Alejandro Cirilo available at <http://tierra-y-vida.blogspot.com/2007/03/message-from-don-alejandro-cirilo-perez.html >

Chapter 5

1. See Aluna Joy Yaxk'in's website <http://www.kachina.net/~alunajoy/2011-march8.html> for further details.

Chapter 7

1. Coleman Barks, *The Essential Rumi* (New York: Harper Collins, 1995).

Chapter 8

1. King James edition of the Bible, John 14:12
2. This descriptive phrase is taken from the books of Tom Brown, Jr. It is the closest description for me of what "God" essentially means.
3. Kiara Windrider, *Doorway to Eternity: A Guide to Planetary Ascension* (Mount Shasta, CA: Heaven on Earth Project, 2001).

Chapter 9

1. Kiara Windrider, *Deeksha: Fire from Heaven* (Maui, HI: Inner Vision, 2006).
2. In the past couple years, some changes have been made within the organizational structure of Oneness University that need to be acknowledged. The initiation fees are no longer so high, and Deeksha initiates are now encouraged to share the training with anyone they choose anywhere they choose.

Chapter 26

1. See Adyashanti's website <http://www.Adyashanti.org>
2. Adyashanti, *Emptiness Dancing* (Boulder: Sounds True, 2006).

Chapter 30

1. King James edition of the Bible, John 18:36

About Kiara Windrider

Kiara Windrider, MA, MFT, spent much of his early life traveling and practicing various spiritual traditions in India. A life-long interest in environmental healing, peacemaking, and social justice led to a dual degree in peace studies and international development through Bethel College, North Newton, Kansas.

Later, he completed a graduate program in transpersonal counseling psychology through JFK University in Orinda, California, and worked for many years at an alternative psychiatric center called Pocket Ranch Institute, which specialized in healing emotional trauma and facilitating spiritual emergence. He received a psychotherapy license (MFT) from the State of California in 1998. He has also trained in various forms of bodywork, breathwork, hypnotherapy, and shamanic healing.

A major interest of Kiara has been understanding planetary and cosmic cycles and their relevance to humanity's journey of awakening. He has approached this study through the eyes of shamans, geologists, historians, physicists, prophets, and mystics. From this research, he has come to the firm conclusion that we stand collectively at the brink of a quantum evolutionary leap beyond our wildest dreams.

He is currently focused on planetary healing using a system of anchoring divine light known as Ilahinoor. His greatest wish is to live fully in the wonder of each moment and to help awaken this beautiful planet to her destiny. He has written four books: *Doorway to Eternity: A Guide to Planetary Ascension*, *Deeksha: The Fire from Heaven*, *Journey into Forever: Surfing 2012 and Beyond*, and *Year Zero: Time of the Great Shift*.

Please visit his websites Kiarawindrider.net, Deekshafire.com, and Ilahinoor.net. Kiara travels frequently and is available for conferences, seminars, and retreats around the world. Suggestions and comments are always welcome and may be addressed to kiarawindrider@gmail.com. He can also be found on Facebook.

Kiara was born on March 6, 1959, at 2:06 a.m. in Bombay, India.

ALSO BY KIARA WINDRIDER

YEAR ZERO
TIME OF THE GREAT SHIFT

KIARA WINDRIDER

Time is *cyclical*, not *linear*. The year 2012 represents both the end of a great cycle of time and the dawning of a new one. Drawing on meticulous research as well as personal shamanic experience, *Year Zero: Time of the Great Shift* clarifies the "big picture" of planetary evolution from the perspectives of ancient wisdom and modern science, revealing an intricate interplay between phenomena (such as galactic superwaves, magnetic pole reversals, evolutionary impulses within matter, and the descent of supramental light) in order to shape a new species of humanity on a rapidly evolving earth. Rather than waiting passively for something to happen to us, now is the time to actively dream a new world awake!

"As I write, I am days, possibly hours, from experiencing the birth of my first child. I can barely contain myself as I implode with gratitude for the gift of Year Zero! Every word resonates on a cellular level, awakening ancient memories and realigning my consciousness with an unshakable knowing that the best has yet to come. This is more than a book; it is a manual for building the new world! A world I am honored to leave to my child."

— Mikki Willis – new father/founder, Elevate

"I read this book twice because it was so provocative and compelling. Kiara Windrider has done something almost no other author has before. He has built an architecture – at the same time both scientific and spiritual – that, better than almost any other book I have read, explains what is going on in our world, solar system, and galaxy today . . . and where this all is going and what its implications for humanity are likely to be. Year Zero is an unusually authoritative, integrated picture of the future!"

— John L. Petersen, Editor of FUTUREdition and author of *A Vision for 2012: Planning for Extraordinary Change*

$16.95 | 211 PAGES | ORDER NUMBER: YEARZERO | ISBN: 9781611250077

DIVINE
ARTS

DIVINE ARTS sprang to life fully formed as an intention to bring spiritual practice into daily living. Human beings are far more than the one-dimensional creatures perceived by most of humanity and held static in consensus reality. There is a deep and vast body of knowledge — both ancient and emerging — that informs and gives us the understanding, through direct experience, that we are magnificent creatures occupying many dimensions with untold powers and connectedness to all that is. Divine Arts books and films explore these realms, powers and teachings through inspiring, informative and empowering works by pioneers, artists and great teachers from all the wisdom traditions.

We invite your participation and look forward to learning how we may better serve you.

Onward and upward,

Michael Wiese
Publisher/Filmmaker

DivineArtsMedia.com

HERE ARE OTHER **DIVINE ARTS** BOOKS YOU MAY ENJOY

THE SACRED SITES OF THE DALAI LAMAS
by Glenn H. Mullin

"As this most beautiful book reveals, the Dalai Lamas continue to teach us that there are, indeed, other ways of thinking, other ways of being, other ways of orienting ourselves in social, spiritual, and ecological space."

— Wade Davis, Explorer-in-Residence, National Geographic Society

YEAR ZERO: Time of the Great Shift
by Kiara Windrider

"I can barely contain myself as I implode with gratitude for the gift of *Year Zero*! Every word resonates on a cellular level, awakening ancient memories and realigning my consciousness with an unshakable knowing that the best has yet to come. This is more than a book; it is a manual for building the new world!"

— Mikki Willis, founder, ELEVATE

THE SHAMAN & AYAHUASCA: Journeys to Sacred Realms
by Don José Campos

"This remarkable and beautiful book suggests a path back to understanding the profound healing and spiritual powers that are here for us in the plant world. This extraordinary book shows a way toward reawakening our respect for the natural world, and thus for ourselves."

— John Robbins, author, *The Food Revolution*, and *Diet For A New America*

A HEART BLOWN OPEN:
The Life & Practice of Zen Master Jun Po Denis Kelly Roshi
by Keith Martin-Smith

"This is the story of our time... an absolute must-read for anyone with even a passing interest in human evolution..."

— Ken Wilber, author, *Integral Spirituality*

"This is the legendary story of an inspiring teacher that mirrors the journey of many contemporary Western seekers."

— Alex Grey, artist and author of *Transfigurations*

SOPHIA—THE FEMININE FACE OF GOD:
Nine Heart Paths to Healing and Abundance
by Karen Speerstra

"Karen Speerstra takes us on a journey of the mind and heart through history, psychology, myth, archeology and architecture; through the width and breadth of time and culture. Hers is a tapestry of words that would have made weavers of the ages proud."

— Craig S. Barnes, author, *In Search of the Lost Feminine: Decoding the Myths That Radically Reshaped Civilization*

1.800.833.5738 • 25% discount available online • www.divineartsmedia.com